THE MAKING OF A BO$$

From 532 to Suburbia

CHELLEY ROY

GetTeaWaisted.com

ChelleyBossUp@Yahoo.com

Quantity sales. Special discounts are available on quantity purchases by bookstores, corporations, associations, and others. For details, contact the publisher at the address above.

Jackson
PUBLISHING
LET THE WORDS CHANGE YOU

DISCLAIMER

This is the past as I remember it.
To maintain the privacy of people still living, in some instances I have changed the names of individuals and places, and identifying characteristics and details such as physical properties, dates, and places of residence.

In Loving Precious Memory of my mother, Deena Lyons. You are my rock and my everything.

In Loving Memory of my grandmother and my Aunt Gerri. Without you, I would not have made it.

For all you young women who have faced fear and turmoil in dark and difficult times, and who have seen many adversities. There is so much hope for you. Stay in the fight, and never give up.

ACKNOWLEDGMENTS

This book would not be possible without my grandmother. I would not be possible without my grandmother. For all that we shall see her in this book as a complicated person, my granny was my security growing up. She was the unshakeable foundation of the family.

She was the one who was always there, in her house, waiting for you. She was the one who made sure I never went without anything. Who provided love, comfort, and support for me during the times when my mother wasn't around.

My auntie Gerri stepped up and filled the void that was left in my life when my mother passed away. She provided the motherly love, support, and guidance I so desperately needed in the years to come. Both women were invaluable in the molding and shaping of me—and of my son, Bernard.

Without them, I would not be whole and of sound mind. I would not be the beautiful black woman that I am, still standing despite the many hits I've taken.

To begin this book was to embark upon a journey,

to provide clarity and to seek closure. To write it was to become a storyteller—the discoverer of my own history. In the course of interviewing several family members for this writing, I have learned more about my mother than I ever knew growing up.

Thanks especially to my son Bernard and my cousins Baby Boy, Andrea Prince, Killa, and Kuwaldha Lawrence for sharing their own memories of my mother with me. I know she's proud of all of us.

And thanks, first and foremost, to my mother herself. She's the reason I live and stand to this day. She's the reason why I grind, work so hard and have the patience, sacrifice, and dedication to win so hard. She taught me that failure is not an option for her Baby Bear and that education was key if you wanted to compete.

In doing my author photo shoot for this book, the wardrobe choices were very important to me. I wanted to exude what I represent.

I AM… POWER, CONFIDENCE, STRENGTH.

I'VE ARRIVED.

With this knowledge comes much more inner peace and joy.

The pink represents all the heart that goes into the hustle, the blood, sweat, and tears beneath all the struggle. The green represents the grind, the taste of success, the rewards of leveling up.

My family has always had both heart and hustle. The

union of the two is complicated, but they must be united. So for me, this wardrobe was a very powerful statement. It shows who I am, the heart and the hustle.

Special thanks to my cousins Baby Boy, Andrea Prince a.k.a. Princess, Killa, and Kuwaldha Lawrence who contributed their memories to this book. May my mother's impact, influence, and memories remain in your hearts forever.-

CONTENTS

INTRODUCTION

Many of you know me as a Diva, The Classy Lady, or Chelley. You know me as a high-class, intelligent Multiprenuer and program manager, or the woman who helps you to look and feel beautiful, and to be your best. But you don't know the whole story of who I am and where I come from.

That's about to change.

The forces that shaped me were not prosperity or ease. My background is not one of simplicity or peace. Instead, I've endured things you may not be able to imagine. Or maybe you can. You'll read here the complicated truth of my mother, and my life—a blend of refinement and street grime unlike any other.

Maybe you know what it's like to grow up without a father in your life. Maybe you know what it's like to lose your mother to violence at a very young age. Maybe you know what it's like to have family members who hurt you and abused you as well as those that help you.

Maybe you feel like you don't deserve any better.

I'm here to tell you that you do. The most flawless diamonds are produced under the highest pressure, and the strongest people are forged in adversity. If you haven't had any in your life, here's a taste of it. And if you *have*—here's hope.

I don't tell this story so that you'll be impressed with me. I tell it so that you'll be impressed with *you*.

So that you will see that no matter where you're starting out, no matter what secret or public traumas you have endured, you can reach the highest heights, have it all, and win!

And so that you will have a little more compassion, perhaps, for people who do things you don't understand, who are different or misunderstood.

What I have done is possible for anyone. If I can come from a vicious street culture to know instead the luxuries of justice, love, self-discipline, and success, so can you. If I can achieve my dreams and grow my faith-driven seeds, so can you.

If I can do this, so can you.

So believe in yourself. Love fiercely, and with your whole heart. And come with me on this journey—through the worst trials our society can impose, and into your wildest dreams.

1

LADY D

My mother was complicated. Like me, she walked in two worlds. Even as she wore suits and reported to work at an attorney's office, she did violence with her own two hands as a queen of the streets. She wouldn't let me follow in her footsteps, but brought that violence into my life. You can't walk in both worlds without them touching each other.

When I remember my mother, I remember her smile and her street slang. She affectionately called me "bitch" as often as she called me "Bear," and she'd "fuck a nigga up" if he messed with me as reliably as she helped me with my homework after school. It was hard to wrap my head around—this refined, loving lady being the same woman who'd stab a bitch with an ice pick if they caused problems for her family.

Everyone remembers Lady D's smile. It was an explosive smile, pearly white teeth flashing in a perfect caramel complexion.

My mother had high cheekbones, natural symmetry, and makeup artistry worthy of the stars. But don't get it twisted. As much as she was glamorous, sweet and tender, she was also the Ice Pick, the Razor Blade, the gun-toting Queen of the Streets. These two ideals lived side-by-side in her.

When I was a child, she'd sit for hours at our kitchen table, sculpting her brows, tinting her lashes—making sure she was almost too beautiful to look at. And when she laughed, which was all the time, you always wanted to laugh with her.

This was the Lady D I knew. This was the side of her she let me see. My cousins, who were often her enforcers, knew a different side of her.

The Lady D I knew was the one who sat with me and told me stories while she cornrowed my hair, making me as beautiful as she was for my appearances at school. The one who sat me down and talked to me like an adult when I was teased or brought home C's on my report card. The one who gave me the best of everything and instilled in me that education was the best thing I could do for myself.

The same sweet woman who told me stories while she did my hair could, in an instant, switch it up and beat my ass if I didn't get good grades and excel in school as expected. She could torture a nigga if she got wind that they'd done harm to one of her people. And then she could talk her way out of legal trouble, knowing the law as well as any lawyer.

Lady D was a sweet and gentle person in her daily life with me. But to my older cousins and on the streets, she was vicious and malicious, a straight-up gangsta, because she had to be. She did a complicated dance, balancing family and the streets. Balancing the money she brought home with the people she brought it home for.

You see, Lady D was a drug dealer. One of the big ones.

I learned this when I was still a small child. Before my first day of school, my mother sat me down in one of our wooden kitchen chairs. She crouched before me so that we were close, and on a level field. Her achingly beautiful eyes met mine.

"Now, Bear," she said, "when you go to school, you might hear some things about me from other kids. I know how cruel kids can be, and I don't want it to come as a surprise to you. I don't want these kids to say things that might hurt you. So I want you to hear them from me first. I want you to know what's true about your mother, and what's not. And I want you to know why I do what I do."

She explained to me that she sold drugs—an illegal job that many people feared. She explained that my classmates might say that she was violent or evil, or belonged in prison.

"I'm not going to prison. And I do what I do for us. I do it so you can have the best of everything. I do it to keep our family safe."

But as my young child self listened to her on this first day of school, she paused. "But, Bear, there's one thing I need you to know."

Inside, my young body was trembling a little. Not because of what she'd said, but because of the tone of her voice. It was the tone she took so rarely with me—the tone that said she was dead serious, that there was a line I'd better never cross.

The look in her eyes was adult-to-adult. The look you give an equal when making a decision with life or death consequences.

"Yes, Mom?"

"You can *never* do what I do. You can never sell drugs on my corner. I'd kill you first." There was finality, almost venom, in her voice. She'd played out the possibilities in her mind, had decided what would *not* happen.

"You are going to go to school. You're going to get A's. You're going to become a lawyer, or a doctor—or whatever you want to be. But you are *not* going to become like me."

She stood up then, and I looked up at her in wonder. To me she was all beauty, all grace, all style. She was the magazine cover image of what a woman should want to be, what the world wanted a woman to be. She moved freely, spoke confidently, loved warmly, laughed loudly. Her anger was a thing of terror, but it only came out when our family was threatened.

How could I not want to be like her?

Years later, I'd live a truth that was almost too hard to bear. I'd learn exactly *why* she wouldn't let me follow in her footsteps, why she'd threaten me with violence first. I'd learn the lesson more bitterly than I could possibly have imagined at such a tender young age.

But then, my mother smiled. It was like the light came back into the room. She was the woman I knew again—the doting mother, the fun aunt who let all my cousins get away with more than their parents ever would.

"Okay, Bear," my mother said. "It's time for school."

My mother was always a puzzle to those who knew her.

Many times from that day forward, she assured me nothing would ever happen to her.

"No one's gonna get me, bitch," she'd boast, leaning back in her chair at the table. "Everybody knows better than to try." And that was true. For Lady D wasn't just feared; she was loved by almost everyone for the light she radiated. She'd kill a man who interfered with her people—but her sense of loyalty ran deep.

As we grew older together, she jokingly promised that she would be there to see her grandson's basketball career go pro. "I'll always be there for you, baby."

That was Lady D's commitment. She'd only had one child on purpose, for one reason. She meant to give me and my child her all.

From my own early childhood well into my son's, I held onto those words. I took them to heart. When she spoke, it was truth. Whatever she said, I believed her unconditionally.

In part, that was because she didn't hesitate to tell the ugly truth. "I throw bricks at the penitentiary so that you don't have to," she'd say. Any business that needed taking care of, she'd do it—outside the law, if possible.

Lady D had every virtue in excess: beauty, brains, courage, love, laughter. She had a frightening amount of strength for such a small woman, and she read more books than almost anyone I've ever met.

For years she worked as a private investigator for a local attorney, who was just as deeply enmeshed in the grime of the criminal underworld as she was.

Conveniently, private investigators didn't need a warrant to perform search and seizure in our home state. So my mother could gather evidence by any means necessary—and it was always admissible in court.

At the same time, she made more money selling drugs and managing sex workers than she did in her day job. Both she and her boss got their day jobs done because they knew the underworld, and had many friends there.

Later in life, I'd realize that my mother took this job

as a private investigator to learn exactly what her attorney knew about how to escape the law. He was just as crooked as she was, and the two of them traded favors. He would intervene if anyone in the family got locked up; she was his eyes on the street.

You're damned right, I know what you're thinking. A PI-slash-drug-dealer? Wasn't that a conflict of interest? I know! But the jobs together made her more dangerous and vicious than either would have done alone.

The mystery of my mother was this: she chose the street life freely. She chose to live by the sword, the blade, the bullet. She chose to risk arrest and lifelong incarceration and other, worse things on a daily basis. She chose to break the law and do violence. She did not have to.

My grandparents were affluent. They were the kind of family that vacationed in Martha's Vineyard.

My grandmother was an educated woman at a time when getting higher education while being a black woman was almost impossible. A child of the dawn of the 20th century, she nevertheless managed to obtain a college degree, and expected the same of all her children.

My grandfather was the hardest worker I have ever met. He dropped out of school to help support his family at the tender age of thirteen, and he worked all his life. But he built wealth, bought a home, married a woman with enough ambition to get a rocket to the moon, and he loved his children dearly.

How, then, did my mother end up doing what she

did? How did their daughter end up stabbing people with an ice pick instead of going to law school?

It might have had something to do with her brother.

Deena, who would be known as Lady D, was the youngest of six children. Being the baby of the family meant she was always behind her siblings on the path of life. She was the last to learn to read, the last to start school, the last to start earning trophies.

By the time she developed a sense of self, it seemed that her siblings had already done everything a person could do on the straight and narrow. There were no firsts left for her to accomplish, no ways left for her to outshine the older kids who had years of experience on her.

Her mother was impatient for her to grow up. My grandmother loved her children, but to her, that meant expecting excellence from them. She hadn't been able to get through life, get her degree, and find a fiercely loyal husband in any other way.

My grandmother demanded perfection. She expected it. And for an exacting mother of six children, it was sometimes easy to forget that the baby of the family was *supposed* to act out more and know less than her siblings.

My mother wasn't the first to feel the bite of her family's perfectionism. Her nearest brother in age, three years older, was my uncle Kool Breeze. And he was ahead of her on the path of rebellion. By the time little Deena started high school, Kool Breeze had found a way to make a name for himself on a path that none of his older siblings had walked: the path of the hustler.

In the 1960s, drugs flooded the streets at an alarming rate. Made more addictive by modern processing techniques—and very lucrative for the home brewer because they could not be sold in stores—drugs became the most profitable illegal business in America.

They also became one of its leading public health problems, killing countless millions of people through addiction and violence. But that seemed a small price to pay to those who were beguiled by the wealth, glamour, and celebrity that was said to accompany the drug trade—for as long as you survived it.

Right up through the 1980s, cocaine use was so rampant among the rich and famous that Eric Clapton wrote a song about the pleasures of the drug. Designer pipes, spoons, and razors were openly advertised in high-fashion magazines of the era.

The reality for black youth on the ground, of course, was a little bit different. There was money, glamour, and power to be had, sure. But there was also police brutality, gang violence, and addiction. A black woman like my mother was a thousand times more likely to be shot for selling the substance than David Bowie's dealer.

Young teenagers were the perfect prey for dealers and distributors looking to recruit able hands and minds. My mother idolized her brother and his "business" success. By hustling, he achieved everything the babies of the family had always wanted: prestige, power, and wealth, all before he turned eighteen.

My uncle Kool Breeze had, at least for a while, outpaced the studious older siblings on the path to financial success and social status.

My mother followed suit eagerly. Her intellect was just as readily turned to strategic distribution and enforcement as it was to getting straight A's. Soon, she was raking in a handsome salary from drug money even as she prepared college applications on her path to law school.

Between law school and the streets, the streets eventually won. My mother was intoxicated by the power that came with operating outside the law. On the street, the law was in her own hands: there was no need to wait for boardrooms, juries, cops, or even a college degree to become a wealthy and well-respected major player.

On the streets, Deena could order a beating or a hit, wield a blade or gun herself, and rake in thousands of dollars without even obtaining a high school diploma. Early on, people cowered at her will. To a teenager, the fact that this career path carried a risk of getting shot didn't mean much.

For a while, it seemed as though Deena had hacked the system. She'd now bypassed her siblings—who went on to careers like U.S. Marshal, nurse practitioner, certified public accountant, and librarian—on the highway to success.

I don't know when my mother realized she'd fucked up. I don't know when she realized that the game was going to kill her. By the time I was in elementary school, she knew that she would never let me follow in her footsteps. But did she know what was going to happen to her? Or did she still think she'd "get out" safely "someday soon?"

In time, she learned what all hustlers learn: that dying by the sword, for them, is not a matter of if, but when.

When did Deena realize that she'd forfeited her life?

Did she feel that my life was in danger, too?

I'd later learn that the same year I started elementary school, my mother gave my older cousins a very different talking-to. She sat them down, boys aged nine and up, at the kitchen table of my grandparents' house. And she said this:

"Family," she said, "sticks together." She looked the boys dead in the eyes, as seriously as she'd looked at me.

"Don't any of you ever leave my Bear alone. You travel in pairs, at least. You go to school with her, you make sure she comes home with you. You go to a party together, you make sure you all leave together. Never lose anyone. Never leave anyone behind."

At a very young age, my cousins already understood why she said this. They already knew danger, and they walked through it every day.

Over the years, the city had deteriorated around my grandparents' once-affluent neighborhood. Now, it was a routine occurrence for children with expensive clothes, shoes, and backpacks to be jumped by other children who wanted what they had. Anyone traveling alone was vulnerable.

One of the essential skills my mother taught her nieces and nephews was how to fight. The best way to stay safe, on those streets, was to show that if anybody came at you, you'd hit them back harder.

Because of my mother's unorthodox work hours, she became the default babysitter for all of my cousins until I was born. She'd pick them up from school, fix them snacks, help them with their homework, and then take them *to* school the next morning. She never wanted them to walk alone.

This domestic of the mom who picks the kids up from school and makes them snacks might seem strange beside the image of my mother stabbing a man with a shiv. But in our world, both realities were true. Defending your family meant doing violence, and even the most violent people had those they loved.

My cousin Killa credited my mother with saving his life—by teaching him to throw a punch. Without the skills of acting fierce and fearless, of "fucking niggas up" when the situation called for it, he firmly believes he never would have made it out of that neighborhood alive.

And Killa knew exactly how powerful my mother was. Years older than me, he was recruited into Lady D's operation before I was born. Before he hit high school, he was helping her to distribute drugs and collect money.

My mother taught him how to act at a traffic stop.

How to hold oneself totally aloof, indignant, even as cops searched the car and you *knew* they'd find contraband.

Once when the two of them were being arrested together, Killa overheard two cops talking.

"Who *is* this woman?" one cop asked the other, shooting a glance at my mother with something like awe in it. She'd comported herself with such dignity and regality, such righteous indignation, that he was still half-convincing himself that the drugs he'd found in her car were real. She projected such a force of will and personality that she seemed capable of almost magically altering the world around her.

"This is the lady I was telling you about," the senior cop said, consulting his database. "The one who runs things down on 8th Street. We've been after her for years, but the charges never stick."

The junior cop shook his head, tearing his gaze from my mother's face with some effort. "She has too much power for one woman. Way too much."

Yet for all that Killa hustled with my mother, learning his skills from her, he did not fall behind in school or drop out like so many young, enterprising hustlers did. Instead, he made straight A's.

The same aunt who taught him how to fight and how to sell drugs also tutored him in math and reading, and demanded exacting academic perfection.

The discipline I'd get later in life—months without

privileges if I brought home a C—was also applied to Killa, and this put him on a path to success in the legit world when he decided it was time to get out of the drug game. Which he did before the events of this book were over, for reasons that will become obvious as you read on.

As Lady D's daughter, I had the most expensive everything. I had a reputation I didn't even know about. And maybe Lady D was worried about more than just jealous kids when she sent me out into the world.

My cousin Kuwaldha Lawrence remembers my mother stopping him on the street one day as he walked home from school.

"Kuwaldha!" she called from the corner. "Come over here! I need you to do something."

Kuwaldha hesitated. He'd been grounded, forbidden by his parents to go anywhere but home and school. And he knew what it meant when Lady D had a job for him. Kuwaldha was a big, athletic boy who had been beating people up on my mother's orders since grade school.

But you didn't just say "no" to Lady D.

"I can't, Aunt Deena," Kuwaldha tried as he walked toward her reluctantly. "My mom said. She'll kill me if I get home late."

"Well, right now, I need you." Lady D brushed his concerns off. "I need you to beat this fucker into the ground for me."

Only then did Kuwaldha see the man—a young

man lurking in the shadows, glaring daggers at Lady D. Competition, clearly. An upstart selling dope on a street corner that did not belong to him.

"But Aunt Deena—"

"I'll get you out of trouble with your mom," my mother promised. And she meant it: Kuwaldha's mother was her best friend outside of the streets. "But I need you to do this for me. Right now."

Cracking his knuckles, my cousin Kuwaldha complied. Not for the first time in his life, he beat a man until that man went running in fear of my mother's muscle.

My mother didn't make the same mistakes her older brother did. My uncle Kool Breeze—once a charming, precocious young man she'd idolized—broke the cardinal rule of the drug trade. He sampled his own product and developed a lifelong heroin addiction, which destroyed him in every possible way.

By the time I was born, my mother was the shining, successful one out of the two of them. By day she was the prettiest, most charismatic, most charming, most attentive mother. By night, she was the baddest bitch to ever sell crack and wield an ice pick on the streets of Washington, D.C.

Her big brother Kool Breeze, on the other hand, was a sanitation worker. He was present for his daughter, Andrea Prince, and sometimes at my grandmother's house he'd sing like an angel, charming women and men alike.

But my mother was the rockstar of the family—at least in my eyes.

Out of all my cousins, aunts, and uncles, it was my mother who could turn heads across the room and command a crowd of people with a glance. Men fell in love with her and orbited like planets orbited the sun. Women admired her as much as they resented her, resenting her at least half because she performed fierce, sultry womanhood more brightly than any of them could.

My mother had no inhibitions. She'd wield her power in any which way—be it by drawing the family children into her drug cartel, or by being more unapologetically beautiful than you thought any human being could be.

She threatened once to kill Kuwaldha's science teacher after the man gave him a failing grade. Kuwaldha had to sit the teacher down and make him understand that my mother was serious, and that he might need protection.

At the same time, she held court at her kitchen table. Men came from miles around to see my mother, to work with her, and more than a few of them fell in love with her.

That, perhaps, is why she shined so brightly. Anything she did, she did with her whole heart, her whole body, the whole force of a loaded gun behind her. She held nothing in reserve. She restrained herself not at all. And so she was the most colorful, the most vivid, the most alive person in any room.

Lady D had carefully made her plans to have me, just like she did everything else. She would have precisely one child, and she would give that child all her love. She would give that one child the best of everything.

Her money. Her time. Her encouragement. Her discipline.

She would give that child the best of everything, and that would make it all worthwhile.

2

SUGAR BEAR

I'm told my dad was a very good-looking man. She dated the strongest and most handsome of the men who congregated around her kitchen table. My mother saw him and knew that the two of them would make a pretty baby, and so, I was born.

I came into my mother's life like the sun breaking over the horizon. I was given the name "Bear" with a hint of sugar added by my grandpa, who loved me and my mother so much.

My father, Bishop, was a good man, with a good family whose stronghold was the apartment complex on Barnaby Street. My mother thought, for a while, that they could settle down together.

I don't have many memories from Barnaby Street.

Psychologists say we forget almost everything that happens to us before the age of three. But the memories I do remember have spellbinding power.

Those early memories are so often more about *feeling* than about specific words or shapes, and I remember the heat of summer days.

The apartment at Barnaby Street had asphalt that could grow blisteringly hot in the summer, when a mystical haze hung over the horizon in the evening. I knew that my mother was well-loved, even then.

I remember seeing her in the parking lot, talking and laughing with my father and other people. I remember hearing people hollering greetings to her across the hot pavement. I remember watching her crouch down to speak to my cousins, who were my age or older, as they played on the street.

I remember my mother, all smiles and laughter, all glamour and beauty. I remember her soft hands on my face, her strong arms picking me up.

I remember my father grinning proudly, a little bit dumbfounded in the presence of my mother and his Sugar Bear, a little bit unable to believe that he had helped create me.

I remember my mother watching *Godfather* movies in the living room. I knew that the Corleones mixed violence and familial affection in a baffling way, and that the shooting of Vito Corleone was "business, not personal." I knew that in their on-screen world, lethal violence was the price of wielding great power.

I did not know how portentous any of that would be for my own life.

And there was a side of my mother that I did not know. I did not know how violently my mother protected me.

The apartment complex was my father's family's stronghold. His own father, his sister, and her children lived there. As the babies on the block, me and my cousins were vulnerable to bullying. I never knew this—perhaps because my mother took care of that problem before it could touch me.

My father's sisters and their father lived in the same apartment complex—one reason my mother had moved there. My cousins roamed and played on the hot asphalt while I was still learning to walk. They were just a few years older than me, so they met the bully first.

The bigger, meaner neighbor boy was looking for any excuse to feel strong, and my young cousins were the perfect targets. When he found he could harass them and frighten them without consequence, he made it part of his daily routine. My cousins began to fear the playground, the basketball court, the hot asphalt. They moved like they were afraid of their own shadows.

As is so often the case with childhood bullies, civil conversations between adults did not solve the problem. The bullying persisted, and my mother knew exactly how much she was willing to take.

One day she invited Kuwaldha Lawrence, a cousin from *her* side of the family, over to play.

Kuwaldha was years older than me, but still in grade school at the time. "Now listen," she told him, before turning him loose on the playground. "You're a big, strong boy. You're so big and strong, I'll bet you could beat anybody up. And I want you to beat someone up—see that boy, there?"

My mother pointed with a perfect, manicured hand out across the asphalt, to where the bully was roaming.

Kuwaldha nodded.

"You don't have to start anything. But if he so much as speaks to your little cousin the wrong way, I want you to kick his ass. Make him regret it. Make it so he'll never give anybody trouble again. You got that?"

Kuwaldha nodded. He went to play with the younger children, as he'd been told. And not long after, the neighborhood bully started shouting mean remarks.

Kuwaldha walked up to him. He wound his arm up and threw all his weight behind a punch so hard, he heard the bully's orbital bone crack under his knuckles.

The bully ran past my mother, clutching his eye and screaming. She smiled in delight. No one at Barnaby Street ever bothered my cousins—or me—again.

I grew up not realizing all the ways in which my mother protected me. But as a toddler, I just knew that I was safe. I didn't know how my mother made sure of that.

I was beautiful, I'm told, even as a child. All children are beautiful, but I was the kind of beautiful that put me in danger too young. I was very much Lady D's daughter, both in bone structure and behavior. I loved to make myself pretty, to charm with a dazzling white smile. I had her warmth, which could be mistaken for flirtation, and which made grown men's hearts flutter at the sight of me.

Lady D made me classy, but she also treated me as an equal. "Bitch," she'd say, "life is rough. You'd better do what I say. I'll teach you how to survive."

Even when I was barely walking, I was just the kind of beauty that made grown men and women stop and marvel at me in the street. I was the apple of my daddy Bishop's eye, and the sole occupant of my mother's heart—just as she'd intended.

As the baby of the family, my mother made sure everyone looked after me. I got anything I wanted. I was allowed to do anything I wanted, as long as I had protection. Which I always had. A small army of older cousins, most of them boys and many already street-hardened, stood behind me. I was the princess of the Barnaby Street block. For a time, I had the good life.

I remember my mother handing me sweets with her blinding smile. "They're made of sugar, just like you." I remember her hands in my hair, and I remember looking up to her incomparable beauty. Sugar Bear and Lady D had to look perfect if we were going anywhere important. We made a perfect pair.

I remember her dancing to music in the living room of our apartment, trying to sing. She may have looked like Beyoncé and possessed the same swagger, but she didn't have the voice. My father would laugh and harmonize as she squawked along to her favorite songs, turning the room into a private party.

I remember vivid glimpses of the hot asphalt, the dusty summer evenings. Of seeing my mother—the most beautiful woman in the world—and my father standing alone in the parking lot, on the porch, on the sidewalk.

There was something of paradise to those early years, like there is for all children. A paradise of innocence, before reality sets in.

My mother and father lived together for only the first few years of my life, before the strain of her fast life and Bishop's career as a truck driver—which meant long, extended absences—became too much.

When they broke up once and for all after four years of partnership, my grandfather was there to comfort his baby girl.

"Come home," he said in his soft voice, looking at my mother with earnest eyes.

If Lady D had any doubts about running her extensive drug ring out of her parents' house, she didn't share them.

"Okay, Daddy," she said, cradling me on her hip. "I'll come home."

Together, we moved into my grandmother's house—and my whole world changed.

3

GRANDMA'S HOUSE

From the outside, life in my grandma's house was idyllic. My grandparents had the perfect life: a nice house, six grown children who'd found different kinds of success, plenty of money to burn (my grandparents used to slip me and my cousins $20 bills—nearly $50 in today's money), and most importantly, good friends.

But the oasis my grandmother created didn't always keep out the violence of the streets. My cousins were still jumped if they made the mistake of walking home from school alone, and my mother's customers and business associates swarmed around our house.

The neighbors seemed grateful: police were not reliable protection in these parts. Being on terms with your local drug lord—or Lady—was much better.

My grandparents and their neighbors, the Strands, were like family to each other. I'd sit on the porch and play with the youngest Strand children while my grandpa and Mr. Strand smoked cigars, talked, laughed, and watched the people who passed by in the neighborhood.

At first, they knew almost all of them. There went so-and-so, whose baptism you'd all attended. He was a bit of a troublemaker, but he had a good heart. There went such-and-such's daughter, who my grandpa and Mr. Strand would holler at to get home before the streetlights came on.

If my mother was around, she'd be less polite. "Crazy bitch," she'd yell out of the living room window. "What you doing down here all by yousself?" My mother literally spoke two languages: street English and business English, each with its own power to communicate. You used business English to communicate stability and peace; you used street English to communicate power and danger.

Like so many black communities, this neighborhood was like a family. Everyone went to the same church, watched each other's children, and shared in personal triumphs, in-jokes, and tragedies.

My grandparents' house was always full of people. Whether it was a few of my dozen-odd cousins, aunts, and uncles or neighborhood kids who had been made honorary nieces and nephews, people who knew the family well came in the back door—not the front—and sat in the kitchen, where my mother was most often holding court.

I remember my mother sitting me down in one of those kitchen chairs to cornrow my hair, making sure I was clean and sharp for school. Lady D took as much pride in my appearance as she took in her own, and I did not complain about the long hours spent with my mother's fingers running gently through my hair while she talked to me and smiled.

She would tell me stories as she worked. Silly stories, children's stories—but always with an element of truth to them. My mother had started her career at age fifteen, and she did not believe that children needed to be sheltered or restricted from the harsh realities of life as much as some grown-ups did.

One of her quirkier habits was her insistence on wearing nothing but a bath towel as she sat at her kitchen table. Even when the cousins brought their wide-eyed teenage friends through, she moved without a care in the world. She wasn't worried about anyone touching her without permission; if someone didn't already know not to cross her, they'd learn soon enough.

I went to nursery school at the nearby church—a building that had once been a row of houses, then connected to each other and filled with pews. My grandmother had been a member of this church for decades, and attended every single Sunday. On weekdays, I'd get on a bus that trundled me up the street to the church, along with all the other neighborhood children too young for elementary school. On Sundays, my grandmother would take me to church with her.

My grandmother dressed up for church the way my mother dressed up for everyday life. She'd wear ornate, impeccable hats, bright colors, flowers. If she was going to go to church, she was going to celebrate God's creation, and that meant wearing as much of it as possible.

My mother never went to church, but she'd send envelopes of cash for the collection plate. I didn't understand the irony of that until later.

When I started elementary school, my mother was the definition of an involved parent. She planned her work around my school days, made sure that she was home when I got home. She'd sit with me while I did my homework, always offering a sharp eye and supportive questions when I needed them.

Throughout my school years, she'd make surprise visits to my school to make sure I wasn't acting out or cutting class. It's amazing how much better you behave in school when you think your mother might pop in at any given time. Especially when your mother is a woman who strikes terror into the hearts of men for miles around.

There were many things I still didn't understand, at that time, about my mother's work. I knew that what she did was illegal, that it might be frowned upon or mocked by others, including students at my school.

Yet I also knew that she was loved by everyone. Lady D was always surrounded by friends, always joking and laughing with the neighborhood dope fiends. She was fiercely protective of anyone she considered family, and was regarded as a benefactor by many.

Although my mother was the most thorough and vicious of hustlers, she had regard and respect for people. If my mother regarded a friend, a dope fiend, or anyone as family, our house was their house. They always had a place to stay. And her viciousness only made her more of a resource: there were powerful parties in town who would not touch my mother's friends for fear of her reprisal.

My granny's house was always spotless. You could eat off the floor, because dope fiends competed in what seemed like a contest to be the first to clean our house from top to bottom. They knew they'd be paid by my mom with some of her good raw hide dope, or some of the white stuff in the small baggie.

I didn't fully understand why she had so much money for the church collection plate, or why she could be home at 3 p.m., but then out late into the night while my grandparents tucked me into bed. I didn't understand why she sometimes spoke in low, hushed tones to the people in the kitchen.

I'd learn later that when she sat at that table, she was as likely to be planning retribution as a business deal. Whenever someone "messed with" the considerable network of people she took under her wing, there would be violent consequences.

At the time, all I knew was that I was in awe of her. She was barely taller than her mother—5'5" and slender, 110 pounds soaking wet. But she radiated strength and vitality, an energy which manifested as seductive warmth or resulted in heart-pounding terror depending on her desire.

My cousins tell stories of seeing her go off on people who had wronged her people in some way.

Once, she terrorized a girl who had told her parents that my cousin Kuwaldha stole from them. He hadn't, and the culprit was later revealed to be a drug-addicted member of their own family. She believed Kuwaldha when he told her this, and was incensed that anyone would accuse her beloved nephew of something as low and dishonorable as theft.

She also didn't appreciate the implication that Kuwaldha needed money.

"My family don't steal from *nobody*," she raged. "They need something, they ask *me*."

My mom was gon' let this bitch know that she did not appreciate false accusations against her family. She went to the convenience store where the girl worked, walked in through the employee entrance, and snatched her ass up by her throat.

My mother choked her ass lifeless and told her not to fuck with her family. Store customers watched in horror, but they couldn't get to her through the bulletproof glass that separated the cashier from the public.

Another time, my cousin Killa was jumped, robbed, and beaten within an inch of his life. His would-be killer left him for dead.

This proved to be a mistake on the assailant's part. When Killa woke up in the hospital and told Lady D who'd jumped him, she went into action.

My mother found the wannabe thug who'd tried to end Killa's life. Pretending ignorance of his role in the crime, she invited him into an alley to sample her latest batch of raw hide cocaine.

When she had the man safely in the dark, she stabbed him repeatedly with an ice pick.

The man came closer to death than Killa had. At the hospital, they called "code blue" as this nigga's heart stopped several times.

Luckily for him, he survived. And since Killa had survived too, my mother called it even. But the incident sent my mother's trademark message loud and clear: it wasn't safe to fuck with Lady D's family.

This wasn't the first time my mother had narrowly escaped a murder charge. Her philosophy was "an eye for an eye," and there was a lot of murder on the streets of D.C.

In this case, it helped that the police had a hard time believing the thug's story. They looked at this 110-pound woman next to the 300-pound man she'd almost killed and shook their heads.

"You're telling me that *this* little woman did this to you? By herself?" I imagine the officer gave a condescending shake of his head. "Unreal. Unbelievable. Call us back when you feel like telling us who really jumped you."

Between the fear of my mother and the street code against snitching, it was a long time before anybody reported her again.

It's difficult to reconcile all of these images, even for me.

You don't expect the same mother who sits with her child at the kitchen table and does homework with her to be capable of stabbing a man repeatedly with an ice pick in cold blood.

You don't expect the same woman who lovingly does her daughter's hair to strangle a woman for accusing her nephew of stealing.

Yet, these contradictions are the most important part of my mother to understand.

Why do people do what they do? What motivates them to enter the drug trade? At what point does violence begin to seem a virtuous response to counter violence against one's own family?

I was told that sometimes in the drug game, it can get gritty and grimy. I was told that it could be bloody, could teach you things you'd wish you didn't know. In my early life, I could not possibly imagine how true that turned out to be.

What I knew as a small child was that my mother was always there for me. She was there for me in a way that many parents weren't there for their children. That she loved me, and found me precious, and there was nothing in the world that she wouldn't do to protect me or for me.

From the outside, at least, we had domestic bliss. My mother's street violence only reached my ears years later, and my aunts and uncles turned a blind eye to it.

The first major blow to all that came when my grandfather died. On that day, my life changed forever.

My grandfather was the glue that held our family together. My grandmother, aunts, and uncles may not have always gotten along with each other—but they all got along with him. He was the first to name me "Sugar Bear," and the one to ask my mother to come home. He was the one no one dared to disrespect—not because they feared him, but because they loved him.

I was very young when the news came that my grandpa wasn't coming home from the hospital. My mother picked up the phone that day and hung it up silently, in a daze. I'd never seen my mother shocked by anything before.

A sort of numbness settled over the house. My grandpa had been my grandmother's husband of sixty years. He had been my mother's rock and her everything, as she was to me. A piece of my mother died that day.

I remember her laying on the couch for whole days out of the weeks to come, sobbing inconsolably. As a child, I was frightened. I didn't know what to do except press myself against her as hard as I could and kiss her, praying I would be enough.

I was too young, then, to understand the crucial role my grandfather had played in my mother's life. I hadn't noticed the cold distance between Lady D and her own mother, or the way my uncles checked themselves, glancing fearfully at their father when they felt they'd overstepped their bounds.

I hadn't noticed the judgmental stares my grandmother gave her daughter, or the fights they got into in hushed tones in the kitchen. I did not realize that my mother had always felt unloved by her own mother, or just how true that might have been. I did not see the barely concealed rage simmering beneath the surface in my uncle's eyes.

With my grandpa gone, everything shifted. The fights between my mother and grandmother became louder. Without fear of my grandpa overhearing, I once heard my grandmother say to my mom: "Well then, move out if you're not going to live the right way!"

"My daddy would never ask me to move out," my mother replied tearfully. "This is my daddy's house!"

The real trouble began when Uncle Strap moved in with us.

Uncle Strap was my mother's brother—a U.S. Marshal and a boxer. Though he was publicly admired for his work as an upstanding enforcer of the law, in my eyes, he was just a bully.

Uncle Strap was a big, mean man. His voice sounded like thunder when he yelled, the kind of voice that would chill your soul.

He moved in with us after a messy divorce with his wife. He was not allowed to see his own children after the divorce, and I think that's part of why he was so violent toward my mother. If he couldn't discipline his own children, he was going to discipline *somebody,* anyway.

He knew about my mother's job, like the rest of the family. And like his mother, he disapproved of it. Neither Uncle Strap nor my grandma could understand why Lady D wouldn't "go straight," or why she'd ever stepped off the straight and narrow in the first place.

Without my grandpa there to protect her, Uncle Strap took it upon himself to try to "beat the devil" out of her.

I remember being shocked the first time my uncle hit my mother. I had never seen such violence, except between children—and my Marshal-boxer uncle was no child. He had the biceps of a bodybuilder, and an adult viciousness about him. My mother seemed stunned, too. She waited for her mother to say something. My grandmother said nothing. She got up and went into the kitchen while the beating continued—in front of me.

Uncle Strap would hit my mother, hard, until she was bleeding on the ground. But she always got up. She never stopped fighting. The more she fought, the harder he beat her.

The beatings continued for years.

I remember watching one day from the kitchen doorway, little child's hands pressed to my mouth, thinking: *Why does she keep fighting? Why doesn't she give up?*

He'd beat her down as many times as she got up. His eyes would blaze with rage, even as hers blazed in defiance. It was a titanic clash of wills—one where it was hard to see the lawman as being in the right.

In those moments, my uncle was everything that was wrong with the law. Everything that was wrong with righteousness. He was willing to beat my mother, to do violence to her, on the pretense of protecting her from her own behavior.

I remember one incident when Uncle Strap was beating my mom, and it had gone on for what seemed like forever. My cousin Baby Boy, who lived with us at the time, had been getting older and taller for years. New to adult strength, he had a lot more courage than I had.

On this day, Baby Boy had had enough. He was tired of the beatings. He was tired of Uncle Strap and his threats, followed by his voice of thunder bullying us. On this day, my cousin Baby Boy pushed Uncle Strap up against the wall and pinned him there.

"You'd better not put your hands on Deena again," Baby Boy said, fierce in his newfound strength.

Uncle Strap tried his standby bullying tactic. "Imma kick your ass boy!" he yelled in his voice like thunder. "You better let me go, or I'm not gonna let you off easy!"

"I'm not letting you go," Baby Boy replied. "And you're not gon' hit Deena no more." He applied a little more pressure to his elbow where it pressed against Uncle Strap's neck.

At that point, my insides were yelling, *YES! Thank God for sending us help. Thank God for Baby Boy!*

At that point, our whole lives shifted. I knew that my mom and I were safe, at least when Baby Boy was around.

There was nothing protective in Uncle Strap's eyes as he hit my mother. There was only anger.

Anger at being disobeyed, at being defied. The same anger he'd leveled at the criminals that he detained on a daily basis in his job as a U.S. Marshal, I was sure.

He told himself it was about protecting her, but it was really about obeying him. He was so incensed that anyone would defy his authority that he'd do anything to prove his righteousness.

After Uncle Strap moved into the house, I never felt safe while my mother was at work. He never hit me, but I was always afraid he was going to.

Once, I remember, I was sitting on the front porch in wistful silence, missing my grandpa, who had once sat with me. The neighborhood was quiet without him, and the house felt dangerous now.

I turned around, and terror surged through me as I saw Uncle Strap's eyes, grinning at me. He was sitting just inside the window—and pointing his gun at me. He'd clearly done it for effect, and now he laughed at my fear.

My grandmother never said a word about my mother's abuse at my uncle's hands. She continued to go to church in her big hats and brightly colored dresses. A chilly silence between mother and daughter prevailed—except when they were fighting.

My grandmother, I'm sure, felt that my mother had thrown away everything she had given her. She'd worked incredibly hard to give her children a good life and keep them off the streets. And my mother had gone into them anyway.

But that was exactly what my grandmother failed to understand. It wasn't *her* life. My grandmother's rage at having her wishes disobeyed had long since left the realm of "protecting her children" and entered the realm of harming those who disobeyed.

But she wouldn't see that. And I, as a little girl, didn't have the words to say it.

My mother made sure I had the best of everything she could give me. I had my own room in the old house, the nicest clothes on the block. I had the best toys, and eventually a phone, a record player, a television. The bargain was this: as long as I got good grades, I got those things. My mother did everything in her power to ensure I had the help and support I needed to learn. If I ever brought home C's, they were taken away.

I couldn't let the hostile environment in the house distract me, even with my grandpa gone and Uncle Strap living in one of the other bedrooms. Even if he beat my mother weekly, I had to make good grades.

I often asked why this was happening to me. Why had my loving grandpa disappeared, and been replaced by a man full of rage and violence? Not until many years later would I understand the concept of displaced anger, that my Uncle Strap had lost his wife and children. Not until many years later would I learn that my grandpa had charged him to be "the man of the house" before passing away, and wonder if *this* is what Uncle Strap thought he meant.

Not until many years later would I understand that maybe, just maybe, he was terrified of what might happen to my mother if she stayed in the game.

But soon, there was another family member in the house—one who would scar me in ways that even Uncle Strap never did.

The house had become a sort of family resting place, its six bedrooms space enough for any aunt, uncle, or grandchild who might find themselves without another home and family. After my grandpa's passing, it played home to myself, my mother, my grandmother, Uncle Strap, and Uncle Kool Breeze.

There were good times in that house. I remember my mother sitting at the kitchen table for hours, tinting her brows and lashes and applying makeup. She'd wear nothing but a bath towel, comfortable as anything, refusing to get dressed until *she* was good and ready to.

I remember my Uncle Kool Breeze gambling at that table, and singing and snapping his fingers as he walked through the house. Between my mother and my uncle, he'd gotten all of the vocal talent. He could harmonize with anyone and hold a note for days.

But the warmth and joy of family life ebbed and flowed around a bedrock of terror.

My Uncle Strap was a bully to be avoided at all costs. In my grandfather's absence, he thought he ran the place. My grandmother was quiet, never objecting to his methods, and out of the house on weekends with her duties as church treasurer.

My Uncle Kool Breeze was often out of the house as well. Between his day job as a sanitation worker, his night life as a pimp, and his big family, he had a full plate. By day he'd be out collecting garbage. By night he'd be driving his nieces and nephews around the city in his shiny Cadillac, blasting good soul music while Andrea Prince, Kuwaldha Lawrence, and Killa rode shotgun.

They'd listen to WHUR, a local radio station at the time, as he drove around checking on his money and his women. The whole family sang along to the songs on the radio, and everyone tried to mimic Uncle Kool Breeze's spectacular voice.

My mother was always home when I got home from school, but her business took her out into the streets on nights and weekends, when the party scene lit up.

On weekends, my cousin Bigelow would come over.

Bigelow was five years older than me. He was just about old enough to know what sex was, and not old enough to have an adult's sense of responsibility. I was not yet a pre-teen.

The adults saw no need to supervise the children—as long as we were in the house, or back by the time the streetlights came on, they expected us to take care of ourselves.

My cousin Bigelow was, as far as I was concerned, pretty cool. He occupied that mystical realm between childhood and adulthood—old enough to look up to, he belonged to that adult-sounding world of "junior high." But far too young to be an enforcer of rules. Young enough to understand kids and their struggles.

Cousin Bigelow would tramp in through the back door of my grandparents' house, through the kitchen and through the living room on his weekly visits. He'd start up the stairs, to where the bedrooms were, and motion for me to follow. He'd go up the stairs first and put his finger over his mouth, telling me to keep quiet. He'd wave his hands for me to follow silently.

I was confused the first time he drew me close and started kissing me. Before I knew it, he was fondling and groping my breasts, putting his hands in my pants to feel between my legs, and sliding my panties to the side to feel me. I was paralyzed.

We were alone in my granny's bedroom. Sometimes he would lay me down on the bed and lay himself down beside me, pretending to talk to me, while he penetrated my insides with his penis.

I can still smell the stuffing on his breath from Thanksgiving dinner. I'd been anticipating some great, grown-up secret when he called me upstairs. The kinds of things older kids shared with you that they weren't supposed to.

But this wasn't what I'd wanted. My cousin Bigelow's slobbery lips all over mine, his penis inside me—I didn't want any of it. Cousin Bigelow took my first sexual experience from me. From then on, any man I was with would be tainted by his memory.

I squirmed. I don't remember whether I pushed him away or protested. I don't remember very much about what happened next, about what kept happening for years. I knew it wasn't supposed to happen. I knew it wasn't right. But I felt like it was my fault, somehow. People always told me I was pretty. And now, I found that I was so shocked, my mouth was frozen. I could not seem to move or say "no."

After that, Bigelow came over on the weekends often. I dreaded his weekly visits, but somehow I always found it impossible to say "no." I was afraid to tell on him. I was afraid, insanely, that he would tell on *me*. I knew that what we were doing—what he was doing—was wrong, but I couldn't get it out of my head that I must have done something to cause it.

When I thought about telling anybody, I saw Uncle Strap's suspicious glare in my mind's eye, the sidelong look he gave me in the hallways. I think somewhere, he thought I was Lady D's daughter—that something was already wrong with me, that I was destined for trouble like my mother. I felt sure that no one would believe me if I told them that Bigelow had been molesting me. Or that if I did, I'd be blamed for it somehow.

A person's mind has a strange way of shutting down when sex abuse is involved. From the very first time, I felt completely paralyzed, powerless to run away. Then that first failure became a sort of weapon I'm not even sure he knew he had: I felt I had to obey him in the future, because if I didn't, *he* might tell.

Even memory has a way of shutting itself down. This was something that did not jive with my self-concept, something I had no way of dealing with. It was something I had to put away from myself.

A person's sexuality has an importance that we often don't understand. At such a young age, I didn't know what sex *was*. I didn't know the word "sexuality," and didn't fully understand why different people had different sets of feelings about the way my mother dressed.

But I saw the power she wielded, the power of my handsome father, a kind of tenderness between my parents that no other adults ever showed each other in front of me. And I knew that something of who I was was wrapped up in all of this: in how people saw me as pretty, as what *kind* of pretty, in how I would change as I grew up, in how

I would wield power and attract tenderness of the same kind.

We don't really understand our sexuality, but I think some part of us does. And I think that's why the mind freezes when it is violated: it is too much to bear.

Only years later would I begin to understand that my first experience with a man had been taken from me, with me too young to have any agency. That many things that should have been sacred firsts were not. The older I grew, the more I understood what had happened to me, and the angrier I became. I knew that I had to write about it.

I hated my cousin Bigelow. We never spoke of it. We didn't speak for years, and whenever I was in his presence, it infuriated me.

Unable to speak, confront him, or tell anyone, I felt embarrassed, ashamed, and violated all over again. I felt like he was undressing me with his eyes at family gatherings, and that felt horrible. It felt disgusting!

I had so much built-up trauma and pain, and I knew I had to put in the work to heal and rebuild my life and my self-worth.

I had to do this work for myself. And maybe for countless other people, once children, who have been in the same position.

It's not your fault. You didn't do anything to deserve it.

I believe you.

THE SMOOTH OPERATOR

I did not know my Uncle Kool Breeze well. I did not know him as my mother knew him, as the fly hustler, the thorough operator, the man whose charm was not merely charming but also fast and powerful. I did not know him as the man people came to when they needed something done, or as the family trailblazer in the drug trade.

I knew him as a happy man. He was made of smiles and laughter, like my mother. Like her, he was considered handsome and charming. He had smooth, clean chocolate skin, a huge pearly white smile, the voice of the Stylistics mixed with the Dramatics, and a good-natured way of winning *or* losing that made you not much mind losing money to him.

But I also knew him as a man who very much seemed the baby of the family next to my mother, the smooth operator.

Uncle Kool Breeze was always a presence in our house. He loved to sing his favorites songs, and he was always on-key. Shawn Colvin's "Diamond in the Rough" would melt into the smooth soprano of The Intruders' "I'll Always Love My Mama" or Bobby Womack's "Across 110th Street." He'd often dance his way down the hallway as he sang, filling the house with music.

But there was a sort of mellowness to his energy. If my mother was a war machine, a tank, a fierce and terrible power, Kool Breeze was a shadow on a canvas. Beautiful, pleasant, good, but never a force of nature.

I didn't understand any of their history. I did not know the reason for his illnesses. I barely even knew what drugs were—only that my mother sold them, and that was bad in some people's eyes and cool in others. I didn't know that drugs could kill you, that drinking could kill you, or about the dangers of anything except smoking, which they always told us about in school.

As a child, I could not imagine Kool Breeze blazing the way for my mother to enter her craft. I could not envision young Lady D becoming the all-powerful Lady D. I couldn't see my uncle, the fast-living wheeler and dealer, sampling his own product.

I didn't know what heroin was, and I couldn't imagine Uncle Kool Breeze using it. Couldn't imagine him slowly losing control of a once-powerful operation, resorting to a legal job for cash, slowly becoming the good-natured sidekick to his little sister. I couldn't see that he was in a controlled fall.

I only knew that my uncle was my mother's friend, and that he was sick.

From my earliest memories, my Uncle Kool Breeze was in and out of the hospital. Although he was only in his early thirties, the doctors said that his liver was failing. During his stays in the hospital, my mom would visit him, taking her little jukebox radio so he could hear his favorite songs by the Stylistics.

My mom didn't pull punches when it came to her brother. She had been barred from the hospital several times for cursing those bitches out at the nurse's station for not being attentive enough or caring for him the way she felt they should.

There were times my mom had to take matters into her own hands by slipping Uncle Kool Breeze some cocaine to help him get comfortable and help relieve the pain. Even if the nurses caught her, she dared a motherfucker to say anything!

That didn't mean much to me as a child. He didn't seem like the sort of sick person you see in a hospital, who's stuck in bed. He sang and danced in the halls at home, held game nights at our kitchen table where a dozen or more local men and women would show up. The men would laugh and joke with him, the women hanging on him, and Kool Breeze with a good-natured smile through all of it.

I never imagined he was dying.

I knew that he went to the hospital once, and came back with his belly wrapped in bloody gauze. I knew that my grandmother, a nurse, had to change his bandages, that they were bloody and they smelled bad. I did not know what it meant when a person with cirrhosis of the liver gets bad enough to need surgery.

He still smiled and beckoned me close, whispering corny jokes with a raspy voice. But he could only use one hand to do magic tricks, now. It seemed a great labor for him to lift his other hand off the bed.

He entered the hospital for the last time when I was a teenager. I didn't know it was the last time, not consciously—but the aura of it hung over the house. In hindsight, I think everybody knew, and I think I felt some sense of finality when he grinned at me before my mother helped him out the door. It's strange how you can know something, and not realize that you know it.

I don't know who took the phone call telling us that Kool Breeze had passed. I just remember walking into the kitchen to see Uncle Strap sitting at the table with a look on his face like none I'd ever seen. For the first time, I could fathom feeling sympathy for the man. He looked haunted. Lost.

Later I would wonder if, perhaps, he felt he'd failed his baby brother. If my mother wasn't the only one he tried to "beat the devil out of." If he was afraid the same thing would happen to her that had happened to their brother

Kool Breeze. If really, part of his rage was worry.

It wouldn't excuse his actions—not for a microsecond. But everybody thinks they're the good guy. Everybody does what they do for a reason. And maybe somewhere in his twisted, violent head, he thought this was the sort of thing that happened if proper order wasn't kept.

My mother was sitting on the living room sofa, her hands draped limply across her knees. She had the same empty, vacant expression she'd had when my grandfather died. I crawled up onto the couch beside her.

"You okay, mama?" I knew she wasn't, but it was the only thing I knew to say.

Lady D took me in her lap. She was still perfectly made-up, perfectly manicured. She still looked like she'd just walked out of the pages of a magazine. She hadn't had time to get disheveled yet.

"No, baby," Lady D said. "I'm not."

She held me for a long time, and I waited for her to start crying. I knew what to expect from when grandpa died. When she finally did, it came all at once, like a dam breaking. She curled around me, sort of tipped over on her side on the couch, and sobbed like a frightened child.

"It's okay, mama," I whispered, stroking her perfect hair. "It's okay."

She was crying too hard to answer, and that was probably good. I imagine now that her mind was so bitter, so full of recriminations. She knew much more about what had killed Kool Breeze than I did, and much more about the world.

Uncle Strap came and stood in the doorway, and for once, I was not afraid of him. Maybe that was because he looked like a different person. There was no menace, no tightness, no tension about him.

Instead, he stood there, seeming almost to waver in the breeze, like a lost little boy turned into a big man. He stared at my mother crying as though he didn't understand what he was seeing, as though he didn't know what to do. He stood there, semi-silhouetted for a while. Then he turned and walked away. I heard his bedroom door shut behind him.

One by one, members of the family seemed to be falling away. There were still countless aunts, uncles, cousins, even boyfriends of my mother. But the core of the family—the people who lived in the house they all came from—were dropping like flies.

A child doesn't have the words to express sadness. They might not even have the words to express fear. They just know that they ache, that things are changing around them, that they don't know what is going to happen now.

Now it was just me, my mother, my grandma, and Uncle Strap in that house. And cousin Bigelow, now old enough to know better, who still visited me and who I was still too afraid to tell on.

With each year that passed, the house seemed to become a more forbidding place. I could feel the tension growing, the sources of warmth and light going out one by one. Now it would be only me and my mother, and all of Uncle Strap and my grandma's rage. My mother could take it, but I wasn't too sure that I could.

I had to get out of there.

Fortunately, I was growing older. Within a few years, I'd be old enough to have a life of my own.

TEENAGE DREAMS

At school, I continued to be the princess. Like my mother, I responded to trauma by becoming more outgoing, more charming—by wielding my own kind of power. By the time I was a pre-teen, I was already *very* pretty. Precocious, my mother would say, like her. I was getting attention from older boys, from grown men.

Despite what had already happened to me, I didn't see the danger in this. I only saw power. Older boys, older men, they had power. If they courted me, if they wanted my approval, then I had it too. Power is a powerful thing to a pre-teen girl who has never had it before.

My mother, as always, saw the danger more clearly than I did. She lived in a world where people took what they wanted, and she wasn't going to give them a chance to do the same to me.

My older cousins were part of Lady D's team. In ways that I wouldn't understand for many years, they helped her. Years later, I'd hear stories from my cousins—of helping Lady D collect money, being her muscle, threatening people for her, helping her operate the bill-stacking machine she bought to package her cash for easy transport.

In my teenage years, my mom would always give me lunch money. But to her, that meant $50 a day—almost $100 in today's money. She wanted to make sure her Sugar Bear had the best of everything, and the prestige to go with it.

I had access to my mom's hoards of cash. My mom had trash bags full of money, and she never hesitated to give any of it to me. After a while, I stopped asking my mom for lunch money. Instead, I would just help myself to one of the many trash bags full of cash.

At one point, my mom had so much cash sitting around the house that she decided to put some of it in the bank for safekeeping. This was during the time before the IRS put a $10,000 daily deposit limit for reporting purposes, so my mom would have me take thousands upon thousands of dollars to the bank and deposit the cash into my account.

I remember like it was yesterday. The walk to the bank was terrifying. It took about fifteen minutes to get from our house to the bank with tens of thousands of dollars in cash on my person. On top of having this kind of cash on me, I was discretely followed by her muscle to ensure her investment—her money and her daughter—made the deposit safely. Being followed should have made me feel better, but instead it drove home to me the danger I was in.

Her muscle included my cousins, some neighbors, and some users who my mother kept close. She'd gather them around our kitchen table and give them strict instructions. And they did what Lady D said, just like everybody in her orbit—not because they were afraid of her, but because they liked and loved her.

I knew danger, but I didn't know how much danger I was in.

One of the instructions she gave my older cousins as I approached puberty was this:

"Don't you *ever* leave my baby alone. You see the way men look at her. You see how innocent she is. I don't want her to be disrespected." She gave the boys a meaningful look. "You hear?"

Our family stuck like glue. Everywhere the kids went, we went in groups. The neighborhood had continued to go downhill around us, and by the time I was in middle school, it was easy for the kid with the most expensive clothes to get jumped and robbed by other children. And that kid was me.

I didn't realize at the time that there were special instructions regarding my safety. I knew that we all stuck together. But I also knew that I had more freedom than my cousins. My mother allowed me to stay out late, to go where I wanted with whom I wanted. And I had the confidence to do it. By my pre-teen years, I knew how to hold court—how to hold the older boys' attention.

What I didn't know was quite how thoroughly my cousins had my back. I was never alone in my wandering.

In middle school, once, I attended an older cousin's basketball game. My cousin Kuwaldha was a local star. Blessed with the family gifts of charisma and the drive to excel at whatever he did, he'd become a little bit of a local legend, a high school celebrity. I was proud to be his cousin—and many of the boys and men were eager to get to know me.

I knew this as they crowded around me, talking sweet, looking at me with shining eyes. I knew this from the subtle competitions they engaged in—still friendly, because I hadn't paid any of them serious attention yet. And I already knew, a little bit, how to hold them at arm's length.

What I didn't know was how quickly things could escalate in this neighborhood. Or that Kuwaldha had been charged with protecting me if they did.

You may have gathered that this neighborhood was rough. You may have gathered that its residents were fiercely loyal to their tribes and families—sometimes more so than was good. On this night, somebody got riled up over the game. Really riled up.

Somewhere in the bleachers behind us, punches were thrown. It soon became clear that this was no teenage-boy fight: it was a grown man who'd turned violent, maybe impaired by something, and other grown men were threatening to follow suit.

My entourage rushed to whisk me out of there. The press of friendly men, their hackles now up, moved me without seeming to move me, out of the bleachers and across the court, which was now empty as the school administrators tried to regain control of the crowd.

Deep inside, I was shivering a little: I was no stranger to seeing fights at school or between children on the streets, but this was different. There was tension in the air, a stink of fear, a sense of total loss of control. It felt like a riot was about to start.

"Bear! Bear!" I heard Kuwaldha calling for me. I hopped up on my toes to see him reaching for me as a coach seized him roughly and dragged him bodily into the locker room. My heart sank a little as the older man shut the door behind him.

As the administrators herded us out into the parking lot and then onto buses, Kuwaldha was pounding on the locker room door. They'd locked the players in from the inside. Kuwaldha nearly lost it with the coach who told him he was not allowed to come watch over me, who promised him that the administration was handling it.

In our family, in our neighborhood, trusting authority wasn't a safe bet. Everybody in my family knew that.

So in the locker room, Kuwaldha was panicking, having just seen me leave in the company of several men. His heart was pounding out of his chest. He crept around the locker room, prying at every loose panel, until he found a back door that the coaches had neglected to lock and sprinted around the building to the parking lot.

By that time, we'd already gone. The administrators, somewhat surprisingly, *had* handled it. But Kuwaldha didn't know where I was or what would happen to me when the bus stopped.

He stood in the middle of the parking lot, feeling empty. Feeling like he'd failed to protect me.

I never knew how well I was protected. I know now, and I wish I'd known years ago. I'd have thanked my mother for the things I didn't even know she did for me. For protecting me from dangers I didn't see.

$$$

I did know that my mother protected family. The street's sense of justice wore off on her, strange beside the suit she wore to her day job as an investigator. Strange beside the regal bearing she wore when she came to watch me and my cousin Andrea Prince perform mock trials at the courthouse.

After passing through the metal detectors at the courthouse, she'd sit, watching imperiously as I out-argued the competition.

Then, afterward, she'd slip back into her real self and slide me a sly grin on the way out.

"What kind of attorney do you want to be, baby?" she'd ask me in a deceptively soothing voice.

"A prosecutor," I said confidently, the first time. Everyone knew it was the prosecutors who caught the bad guys, who got justice for the victims.

Lady D's demeanor changed. "A prosecutor?" she asked, too soft for the other families to hear. "Bitch, you want to put your mama in jail?"

"I mean—a defense attorney, Mama. I'm gonna keep you out of jail."

She'd smile that explosive, pearly smile then. "Oh baby, you gon' make me proud. You keep people *out* of prison. Lots of people just doing what they got to do. You keep them free."

My mother's idea of justice, of course, didn't rely on the law. Hers was a world where nonviolent drug offenders often did more time than rapists and wife-beaters, where victims often feared going to the police lest their own drug habit or sex work land them behind bars. She didn't trust the courts to get her family justice. Instead she trusted her own fists, her own knives, her own guns.

Once when I was in high school, yet another cousin was grabbed off the side of the road coming home from school. He was robbed, beaten, and left for dead—by people who thought they had to kill him to keep their identities a secret.

It didn't work. My cousin woke up in the hospital, and lived to tell Lady D who had almost done him in.

When my mother got wind of this, to say she was

"livid and pissed to the highest of pisstivity" was an understatement.

She called in her muscle and set her plan into motion. She'd show everyone that this was the wrong family to fuck with. She'd do this as many times as was necessary.

She didn't kill the niggas, but I know they wished they were dead. She pistol-whipped each of them, tied them to chairs with plastic bags over their heads, and tortured their asses for hours. She made sure they knew that if anybody harmed Lady D's people, there'd be nothing they could do to protect themselves.

She left them as near to death as they'd left my cousin, and called it even.

I was not supposed to know these things. Lady D wanted to protect her Baby Bear. But word got around to me anyway. Children hear things, know things that adults try hard to keep secret.

As I grew older, my mother saw less need to protect me. But she made damn sure I didn't follow her down the path she'd taken. Education was everything to her, when it came to me. She wanted all the doors that she'd walked away from to be open to me. She wanted me to do great things.

The one time I brought home a "C" in English, my mother beat my ass and cursed me out. She couldn't understand how someone who was born and raised speaking English could get a "C" in English while getting an "A" in a foreign language.

She punished me for months, taking away my television, phone, and CD player, and forbidding me from seeing my friends or going out after school hours. Just like she did with everyone, she made sure I felt the pain of failure. It was the only way she knew to stop me from jeopardizing my academic future.

Only my cousin Kuwaldha was eventually able to prevail on her to have mercy. He convinced her that maybe, just maybe, I'd do better in school if I was allowed to see my friends once in a while.

To this day, I'll never know what Kuwaldha said to my mom. She trusted and believed in him in a way she trusted few other people. He'd been in on her operation since before I was born. He had a way with words with her—no one but him could ever get her to change her mind or let me off punishment.

We all knew how serious she was about my education. She wanted me to have the freedom of the streets, but she'd lock me in my room if I wasn't excelling academically to the level that she knew I was capable of.

When I was excelling, though, I think she figured she had a little leeway. She planned to transmit justice to my cousins and me as a value, even if it meant bending the rules a little bit.

I'd just gotten my driving learner's permit and taken my grandmother's car on a few anxious, tremulous drives around the block. My mother never had a driver's license herself; by the time she turned sixteen, she could pay chauffeurs to drive her from place to place.

In business, she was Lady D. Always with the nicest, newest cars, always with the most handsome and menacing drivers. She was royalty and she wasn't going to let anybody miss that fact.

In personal matters, though. Well, she didn't like to mix family with business. So when the family needed justice done and the task required a car, guess who she called?

One of my first times behind the wheel, I was a getaway driver.

It happened like this: My cousin Andrea Prince had a boyfriend, and the two of them had a child together. They hadn't married because of his philandering ways, but he was helping to raise their baby while he swore to be on good behavior.

Andrea Prince, however, had learned otherwise. She called my mother crying one day. She had learned that he was sleeping with another woman *while* their daughter was in the house. All while claiming that his heart belonged to Andrea and Andrea alone.

She was afraid of her daughter seeing the vicious enforcer that she had become, following in her aunt Lady D 's footsteps. She didn't want her baby to see her busting out windows, or carrying hammers intended to take out her baby's daddy. So she called my mother, knowing Lady D would take care of it for her.

But she was also worried that if she tried to leave him, her boyfriend might not give her baby back. The man had been clear that he felt entitled to stay with Andrea and felt entitled to his child, even if he didn't abide by the rules of their agreement.

Andrea Prince didn't want to call the police. She and my mother both had seen black people get shot by the police at domestic house calls—and not always the person who actually posed a threat. The cops just seemed to get trigger-happy. They weren't to be trusted with a case like this.

Fortunately, Andrea had Lady D.

As far as Lady D was concerned, she *was* the law. She got a squad together and went to work.

My mother was a small woman. I always feel the need to emphasize this, because it was so extraordinary to see her in action. When I saw small women on the streets—my friend's mothers, the other girls at school—they were rarely forceful. They wouldn't get up in your face or curse out and threaten grown men. And if they did, the grown men wouldn't listen. Like the cop who heard the ice pick story, they'd laugh.

But my mother was 110 pounds of pure fire. If she focused like a laser on you, it didn't matter if you were a 6'3" 330-pound man. You were going down.

I watched big men bow down in fear of my mother, and I admired her. I was so intrigued by what she did—how *did* she do that? How did a little slip of a woman, no larger than my grandma, command a significant portion of D.C.'s underground territory? I wanted to learn from her.

And this, it seemed, would be my chance. But I didn't react the way I'd hoped I would.

Instead of assuming Lady D's regal air of command, I got trembling-scared.

"He's in there with that bitch." My mother pointed to the boyfriend's house on a subway map. "He has the child with him, so we have to be careful. Nobody is exposing my grandbaby to violence."

The child wasn't really her grandbaby—more like a second cousin once removed, or something—but in Lady D's eyes, all the family's children were her children. "But nobody is cheating on my niece, either," she finished resolutely.

My mother eyed the other women around the table. All women, family and friends. She didn't want to bring any of her men into this, because it was family business. And I could see unspoken understandings pass between them. That told me two things: they knew exactly what level of violence to use, and they had done this before.

"Bear." My heart almost stopped when she looked at me. The reaction shocked me. It was as though I was seeing a different woman now. I understood for the first time the meaning of "Lady D."

This woman was not young Deena Lions, but some

sort of lethal and dangerous creature. I felt as though a crime boss had called my name—not my mother.

"You're just going to drive." I tuned back in just in time to hear my mother finish her instructions to me. "You can do that. Right?"

I nodded numbly, my mouth dry. My heart was hammering in my chest, my palms sweating.

Were we really doing this? What were we going to do? Why? Was it really necessary? Was this what my mother *did*?

Without a word, I followed my mother and her posse out into the driveway. I opened the driver's side door, got into the car, and turned the keys in the ignition.

The car sputtered to life. The cargo around me—three grown women, dangerously solemn and silent, hammers and ice picks in their hands—felt like I was shipping bombs.

But my mother was there. And I always had to do what my mother said. She wanted what was best for me.

We drove with the headlights off, the old car hiccupping and rattling a little bit on the poorly kept streets of the D.C. neighborhood. Around us, the houses were quiet. The air outside the car was the air of a normal evening. Kids played in yards, old men dozed on front porches with beer cans and cigars. Women slept in their beds or changed their babies inside houses.

But the atmosphere inside the car was the atmosphere

of a military vehicle. Every person was coiled, ready to spring.

My mother stopped us in front of a small bungalow like any other. The windows were dark, and I didn't see any cars in the driveway. I thought to myself: *Are they even here?* But I couldn't speak. Privately, I hoped the targets were not home. I wasn't sure I'd be able to drive back if I saw somebody get beaten down.

I parked the car, shaking along with its tired old body as I shifted the clutch. In near-silence, the doors opened and shut again, three grown women getting out and striding with dangerous purpose across the unkempt front lawn.

The first scream, when it came, nearly made me jump out of my skin. It took a moment for me to calm my hammering heart—it was my mother who had screamed. A scream of rage, not a scream of pain.

She broke one of the front windows. Andrea Prince and one of her best friends circled the house, busting out the windows with hammers and baseball bats. When all of the house's windows had been shattered, they moved on to busting out the windows of the boyfriend's car, where it stood parked nearby.

I watched as the women expertly used ice picks to flatten the tires, inflicting every possible kind of damage. With the car more or less totaled, they all went around the back of the house. Then the night was a chorus of howls of rage and hollered threats, accusations of infidelity and demands.

One thing was for sure: if I were that man, I would never cross my girlfriend or her family again. In fact, I would give the baby to her mother and hightail it out of state, never stopping to look back.

I glanced around the darkness, anxious and amazed by the silence on the street. None of the neighbors had come out of their houses—I wouldn't if I were them. But most remarkably of all, there were no police cars. No more sirens than the usual background noise of D.C., distant howling every few minutes. None of them approached the house as my mother and her friends ravaged the place, making sure its occupants would know they were outnumbered.

It seemed an eternity of breaking glass and full-throated cries before my mother approached the car again, smiling a little satisfied smirk. Her hips swayed the way they always did when she'd just gotten the better of somebody. She'd gone in all business, but came back all pleasure. She pulled open the passenger door with a little flourish and slid into it.

"Drive, baby," my mother said, and I pulled back on the stick with shaking hands.

I drove us all the way home in the bizarre quiet of the night. The neighborhoods we drove through either didn't know what had happened, or didn't dare to do anything about it. The women in the car were still quiet, but this time it was a sort of satisfied silence. Contented. The problem, they were sure, had been taken care of.

I was just as sure it had been handled. But I was less sure how to feel about it. How would I feel if that were my son, my daughter, my grandchild?

I knew that the police often shot or arrested the wrong people, often punished the innocent—but would I rather they had handled it? How much faith did I have that these women, driven by rage and family pride, had control of themselves?

What if the other family decided to hit back? Where would the cycle end?

I did not say any of these things as I drove with shaking hands through the darkened neighborhood and back to our house. I stayed silent until we pulled back into the familiar driveway of my grandfather's house, silent and ordinary as always, and my mother and her allies calmly walked back inside, laughing and chatting softly with each other. I walked in with them, not wanting to look weak, and just sat on the living room couch recovering for the better part of an hour.

My grandmother learned or suspected what had happened.

"Bear," she frowned, tottering into the living room, "I'm surprised at you. Why would you agree to help with a thing like that? You could have gotten in real trouble. You could have ruined your chances."

My mouth was still a little dry. "I've got to do what my mother asks me, don't I?"

My grandmother shook her head, that old familiar look of disapproval on her face. And inside me, fear was replaced by something new: resentment.

Who was she to criticize me, while she was letting Uncle Strap bring worse violence into her house? The anger, the resentment, made me a little bolder.

"Besides," I said, "family's got to look after family."

My grandmother turned around and walked away.

And I was left with my heart thrumming in my chest, adrenaline and anger and confusion mixing in me.

I wanted to make my mother proud. I wanted to be like her. I wanted to learn to wield fire and steel the way she did, to be loved and respected the way she was.

But not like that. My mother had been right: the path she walked was not for me. And now I understood that I didn't need her punishments to keep me off of it. I, too, would do anything to avoid it.

In times like that, I tried to make my mother proud. Tried to show her that I was made of sterner stuff. That I was fearless, like she was.

My cousin Kuwaldha said to me once: "Lions don't scare. It's just not something we do." But I got scared. I had enough fear to keep me on the straight and narrow. To stick to the safe path.

And that's how Lady D wanted it. She always loved me just the way I was. She always told me that. She didn't want me to be different.

She didn't want me to be like her.

6

MY BABY DADDY

Like any teenage girl, I dated my fair share. Lots of men were interested in me—but not many held my attention. As Lady D's daughter, I could date anyone I wanted—but I found few who had what I was looking for. I had my mother's taste for power and influence—but also a taste for the quiet, thoughtful type that was all my own.

The best of both worlds met in a fellow student named B.J.

B.J. was the envy of the girls at my school. He was very handsome, very fit, very fashionable, and he always wore the latest designer threads.

Like me, he seemed to have the best of everything. Unlike me, he seemed to have gotten it for himself. Everyone knew he was a hustler—that was the only way a boy my age would have those clothes, that car, that air of quiet authority.

But there were other hustlers. What set B.J. apart was the "quiet" part. He commanded respect and turned heads wherever he went—but he never flaunted this ability.

He rarely spoke. When he did, people listened. While other hustlers put on shows, gathering women around them, B.J. hung back around the sidelines, watching and making inscrutable calculations behind his beautiful brown eyes.

The very fact that he *didn't* court attention made everyone want him more. It made them wonder what he knew that they didn't. No one knew what he was thinking, so they all assumed that it was something profound.

It made him a sort of king—more powerful for being inaccessible.

I admired B.J. from afar. A man who could handle himself, who could handle a great deal of business—yet who still knew how to hold something back, that was my kind of guy.

I imagined that behind his eyes was a deep, thoughtful soul like my own. I imagined that his restraint was my own kind of discipline. He handled business like my mother, sure. But he was also destined for greater things.

And to my surprise, he felt the same about me.

I wasn't a party girl, as you might have guessed. Being my mother's daughter, I was dedicated to my books. I was sort of the Hermione Granger of my classes: the one who knew all the answers, who was on good behavior to the point of frustrating my classmates who were eager to explore the secret, forbidden world of adult power.

I didn't share their fascination because I had a clear window into that world. It was no mystery to me. Sharing a home with my mother, with her activities, left few secrets. And so I wasn't as intrigued by sex, drugs, and money as the rest of them were. Like B.J., I went about my business quietly, needing nobody's approval.

Perhaps that's why he liked me.

I was as surprised as anybody the first time I looked up to see B.J. standing by my locker. He'd stopped, clearly waiting for me to shut its door. He looked at me with those eyes—dark, mysterious. Never demanding, never giving anything away. Then he asked, in a soft voice, if I would like to see a movie sometime.

I'd be lying if I said my inner schoolgirl didn't jump up and squeal.

But on the outside, I only returned a soft smile and agreed, just as slyly and strategically as he'd asked.

Going out to that movie with him, I felt like a princess. He paid for everything and treated me with the utmost respect. Afterwards, we shared a thoughtful conversation.

Here was my Prince Charming, and he was everything I'd ever wanted.

Our affection grew slowly. Like all slow burns, it was

explosive when it came to a head. The very fact that we were so well-matched—that we both held most of ourselves in reserve—made it impossible to stay away from each other. Made it easy, too, to imagine a future together.

My book smarts and his street smarts—maybe we were the ultimate power couple.

Maybe with my help, he could win the game my mother was so good at playing. And maybe I could give his baby a mother who was a lawyer, as my mother could have been. Who would keep her baby's father out of prison, make sure he got straight A's, and ground him for a month if he ever brought home a C in English.

To B.J. and me, it seemed like we were winning the game. But there was a dark side I never let myself fully understand.

When our relationship was new, I was B.J.'s queen. He treated me the way I thought he should—spoiling and lavishing me, buying me any and everything under the sun. He held doors for me, praised me, and canceled plans with his boys to be with me.

But over time, things began to change.

It was just a little bit of unease I felt at first—doors closed too quickly and too hard, moments when his silences seemed hostile and distant. I'd feel guilt, too, at having caused his irritation. And I didn't recognize that, right away, as the red flag that it was.

When I wasn't available every moment of the day—

whenever he wanted me—he'd grow angry and passive-aggressive. If he felt I was the light of his life at times, he was just as ready to accuse me of ruining his life when I didn't do exactly what he thought I should.

First, it was an exchange of angry words. Recriminations. Questions. Accusations of cheating.

I was so shocked the first time he accused me of seeing another man, I was rendered speechless. I had never even thought about it. But this soon became a recurring theme. If he didn't know where I was, he assumed the worst.

He said he couldn't help it. He said he just *worried* so much about losing me.

When he started hitting me, I told myself the fights were two-sided.

I shoved him back, didn't I? Like my mother, I didn't stay down when I was hit. And I had seen my mother's own brother hit her. So our relationship couldn't be so bad, right?

As the months and years passed, things got worse so slowly that I almost didn't notice. B.J. was effectively controlling me with his rages, his threats, his silent anger. I told myself this was just what passionate couples did. I couldn't leave him. He needed me too much. And I needed him.

He would vanish for days at a time, growing hostile when I asked him where he'd been. Yet if I failed to answer the phone for just a few hours, I could expect a round of hurtful accusations about my loyalty.

Once, I remember, we were arguing in the bathroom at his house. He was angry that we hadn't gone out to dinner together the night before because I'd chosen to hang out with my friends for once.

As with every time I went somewhere without him, he began to accuse me of cheating on him. He seemed convinced that I was seeing another man behind his back.

I had just arrived at his house. My mother had just paid for me to get my hair done at Sweet Sensation hair salon—a very popular hair salon in the city back in the day. If you weren't getting your hair and nails done here, you weren't considered fly at all.

As I tearfully told him the truth—that there was no other man—he poured water onto my hair to ruin the stylist's work. He snatched the bamboo and gold earrings I'd purchased with my name on them out of my ears.

Then, out of nowhere, he pulled a gun. I was paralyzed.

In my mind I saw Uncle Strap, pointing his U.S. Marshal's gun at me from inside the window. That was such a chilling moment, more so because my uncle had been smiling.

As I stood paralyzed with fear, B.J. struck me across the face with the butt of his gun. I heard a bone crack, and felt my blood run cold. My eye and cheek exploded in agony.

There was a thought in my mind that I was in too deep

with the wrong man. A thought that everything about the life I'd known for years had changed.

If he was willing to pull a gun now in his fear and insecurity, he might pull the trigger someday.

I had to get out—but could I do it? Did I even want to?

And there was another thought, just as terrifying.

If my mother ever found out about this moment, she would kill him. I was sure of it. My mother had taken lives for less than this, and I was sure that the police would never find his body. Or his killer.

So not only did I have to leave him—I couldn't ask her for help doing it.

When I came home with a swollen face, I lied about where my bruises came from. My mother suspected, I think, but perhaps also suspected why I lied. She didn't interfere because I didn't ask her to. She trusted my judgment in a way that I no longer trusted hers.

But was she right to trust me in that way? After three years with B.J., I no longer felt that I could see the future clearly. Now, it felt like I was flying blind.

I knew he was not the man I wanted him to be—but I could not see my way out of this relationship. I couldn't imagine another man loving me as much, or me loving him.

I could still see, sometimes, through the haze, the

future I'd once imagined. I could see B.J.'s potential, what he could become if he changed. I could see what *we* could become if that impossible thing happened, if he became the man I knew he could be if he wanted.

But most of all, I couldn't see any *other* future. I could not imagine my life without him. I could not imagine anyone better coming down from the heavens and scooping me up. I had my prince—even if he was a deeply broken prince—and I could not imagine going back to walking my life path alone.

So I stayed focused on that future I could sort of see. Even as it receded into the distance and was covered by fog.

$$$

B.J. and I had been dating for four years when my pregnancy test came back positive. I stood in the bathroom of my grandpa's house, gripped by a turmoil of fear, confusion, and hope.

Fear: what was I doing, bringing a baby into the world with this man? In this *relationship?* What was I doing, bringing a baby into this world without a college degree, and without being married?

My family had made it perfectly clear how a responsible woman brings a baby into the world: when she's older, when she has a career, and on purpose.

Confusion: what would I do now? What would my baby's father do when he heard the news? He'd be happy—

wouldn't he?

But he "loved" me, and look at how he treated me. I couldn't possibly leave him now. I couldn't leave him ever, now that I was pregnant with his child.

Or did my pregnancy make it imperative that I leave him? Did it make it absolutely necessary?

Hope: I wanted this baby. I'd always known I wanted a baby, the way my mother wanted me.

I even sort of wanted it to be *his* baby. I often fantasized about my child being named after his dad, and growing up to have his father's best qualities.

Could I raise a baby with his strong, quiet spirit and his mother's sense of right and wrong? Could I raise a baby with his grandmother's brains and his great-grandpa's heart?

Then, fear again.

I'd have to get through a nine-month pregnancy before I could deliver this child. And B.J. wasn't going to make that easy.

By the second trimester of my pregnancy, B.J. was in prison. I was afraid and disappointed, but not surprised. He'd been in and out of juvenile detention for most of our relationship. Unlike my mother, he didn't seem to be very good at avoiding getting caught.

And even then, I wasn't ready to bail on him. Even then, I could see our future through the fog.

He told me he needed me, now more than ever. He promised that soon, it would all be sorted out.

I wanted so badly to believe him that I just *did.* I wanted so badly to have the future I had first envisioned for us that I had to believe that it was possible.

I used to go out to see him once a week. Twice a week, if I could. Daily visits weren't an option, because of the commute: it was an hour's bus ride to the prison shuttle's pickup point, and another hour or more to actually see my inmate.

Visiting my child's father in prison showed me a whole new world. It wasn't one I wanted to be part of.

Despite my mother's profession, I'd never visited anyone in prison before. I'd had no idea what that side of life was like. And I'd imagined that *my* family was safe from it. Any charges filed against Lady D never stuck.

The prison shuttle was depressing enough as it was. More than ninety percent of its riders were women: mothers, partners, sisters, daughters. More than ninety percent of us were black.

More than a few were heavily pregnant, and I tried to imagine that. I wasn't showing much yet, my baby's birth still a distant prospect for me, and I tried to imagine making the trip out here knowing that my little one was due to arrive at any moment.

There was an air of resignation in the shuttle bus. Nobody *wanted* to be there, but many of us had been many times before.

B.J.'s father, I'd learned recently, had spent almost his son's entire life in prison. B.J. himself had been in and out of juvie before his current incarceration, and now I wondered if this was what I could expect. An eternity, a lifetime, with my father's child in and out of prison?

The experienced women knew what to do when we got off of the bus. They knew not to stick too close together, or talk too much. They knew that their bags would be checked, that their bodies would be frisked and shaken down. It was less to prevent contraband—that was almost impossible to do, one woman told me—and more to humiliate us. To dehumanize us.

We weren't members of the general public that the guards were meant to serve and protect, after all. We were the wives, daughters, mothers of the enemy. We were in bed with the enemy.

It continues to bother me how almost all of the inmates I saw in that prison were black. I knew enough—just enough—from my mother's business, from B.J.'s, to know that as many white people were users and suppliers as black people. Drug purchasing was one area of life that didn't seem to discriminate, and that was what half of the inmates here were in for.

I wondered if they kept the white prisoners somewhere else. I wondered if it was nicer than this. If their families were treated better when they came to visit.

I'd sit across the glass divider from B.J. and talk to

him on the phone. His moods swung wildly.

Some days he'd be the mellow, mysterious man I'd fallen in love with, asking about me and the baby like a good father would. Other days he'd be angry, jealous, paranoid, convinced I was sleeping with another man or that I was going to leave him. He'd threaten me.

I didn't even understand some of his rants—rants about his business, a thing he'd never let me in on before, and which I refused to have any part of.

I knew one thing with dead certainty: I wasn't going to lift a finger to help B.J. with his business. My baby wasn't going to have *two* parents in prison.

B.J.'s incarceration turned out to be a blessing in disguise for me. Although I spent months acting as the faithful partner, worrying for him, for our future, getting on those buses to try to give comfort to a situation I couldn't change—those months gave me the distance I needed to realize that our relationship was wrong.

If B.J. couldn't stay out of prison for me and his child—if he couldn't even do that—what *could* he do for us?

If he could not even reliably be kind to me when I'd traveled two hours to visit him, when I'd endured the humiliation and the hopelessness of the screening process, how could I expect him to treat me when he got out?

I wanted him to be free. But as my belly grew and my baby kicked and his father wasn't there to feel it, I didn't want him to be mine anymore.

When the day came for Bernard to be born, I was surrounded by love and support. But it came from my family, not from Bernard's father. B.J. was in a different penitentiary by then, almost a state away. But my mother, grandmother, aunts, and cousins were there with me.

As I brought that glorious, perfect little baby into the world, my own world changed forever.

I knew, as I held Bernard in my arms, that I would not take him to any prison. I would not take him to see his father incarcerated and ashamed, to see his father walking down a path Bernard could too easily follow.

I would not see my baby become one of the countless men behind bars, being visited by sisters and lovers and mothers for following in the footsteps of their role models.

I knew then that B.J. and I were through. But I didn't know about the last surprise he had for me.

Little Bernard was barely a month old when the phone call came. My mother picked it up, resplendent as usual, wrapped in a towel as she tinted her eyelashes at the kitchen table. Her passion for making herself over meant that she was usually the one to pick up the phone. This was the early 90s, the days of landlines, and ours was next to the kitchen table.

"Hello?" A pause. The pause was too long, I could tell even from my bedroom, and there was something apprehensive in it. "I'll get her. Bear!"

I darted out of the bedroom before my mother's hollering could wake little Bernard. I closed the door softly behind me and scampered into the kitchen.

"What?" I hissed, whispering as loud as I dared.

"Telephone." My mother held the phone out to me and then, diplomatically, turned away. Looking back, there was a sort of grimness in her face as she did it, a sort of purpose as she looked away. I wonder if she wanted to give me privacy. I wonder if she knew what was coming.

"Chelley?" It was my good friend Rhonda's voice on the other end, but there was something wrong with her voice. She sounded nervous. Like something was wrong. Really wrong. "Chelley, there's... something you need to know."

My blood ran cold. My palms began to sweat. I was all ears. My mind raced, thinking over what Rhonda could possibly have to tell me. Had something happened to B.J.? He was in the prison upstate—even if it had, how would Rhonda know first?

"Well, Chelley... there's this woman. And, she just had a baby. Not you. Another woman. She just had a baby. And…"

An inkling had begun to form in my mind, but it seemed completely impossible. What could this other woman have to do with me? Surely not…

"And the baby is B.J.'s." The words exploded out of her like they'd been trying to escape for some time. "Bernard's got a half-brother, Chelley. B.J. was seeing both of you at the same time."

The world seemed to stop turning for a minute.

On one hand, the news was too absurd to be believed. Didn't B.J. always tell me I was his one and only? That I was his princess, and we fit together as no one else did?

And yet, didn't he disappear for days, weekends at a time? His constant insistence that I was cheating on him—why did he believe that? Could it have been because *he* was cheating on *me*, and he was terrified that I would follow his example?

All at once, the pieces fell into place. Another woman. Of course. That explained so much.

And yet, it was impossible.

The phone cord stretched, and I didn't notice I had crumpled to my knees until my mother knelt down beside me. I hadn't said anything. Rhonda was waiting, the dead silence on my end stretching into eternity.

"I... are you sure?"

I had to ask, and yet her answer almost didn't matter. Now that she'd said it, now that she had raised this possibility, *I* was sure. The way he treated me—it would have been more surprising if he'd been faithful, really.

And yet. And yet.

"I've got her number, Chelley." Rhonda sounded tired. "In case you want to... you know. Talk."

"Give it to me." I was scrambling, then, for the pen and the little pad of paper we kept on the counter by the phone. I wrote down the digits one by one, painstakingly, and her name.

When I hung up the phone, my mother was watching me with big eyes. My whole body was shaking, but strangely, I didn't know how I felt.

Devastated? Numb?

...hopeful?

"You alright, baby?" My mother's hands were held out, as though she wanted to touch me but wasn't sure if she should. As though she didn't want to interrupt whatever was happening inside me.

"I... yeah." I knew in that moment that I'd need to cry. A lot. Into my mother's arms, probably, sobbing into her chest as she had once sobbed with her body wrapped around mine when her father passed away.

I would grieve for a relationship that was never what I'd thought it was, for the man I loved who had never really existed.

But not right now. Right now, I had to do something.

I went into the bedroom I shared with Bernard and stood over his cradle.

He looked so peaceful, sleeping in the darkness. I thought of another little boy and of another woman, who was just as scared and abandoned right now as I was.

"Hey, baby," I whispered. "You've got a brother."

7

ALONG CAME MARQUIS

There's a question we ask ourselves often: "Why is she with him?" Why do women who have everything going for them often choose the wrong man?

One answer is cliché, but it's often true: if a woman didn't have a father in her life, didn't have a man who modeled *good* relationship behavior, it's easy to be confused about what that's supposed to be.

When you spend your life looking for your father, waiting for his approval, wondering what you did wrong to make him stop coming around—it's easy to have the impulse to do anything to please other men. Anything to get their approval.

In hindsight, that's what happened to me. I never would have said that that was why I was with B.J., if you'd asked me. I never would have said my attraction to him had anything to do with my father.

But that's kind of the point. I didn't know *what* a relationship was supposed to look like. Not the kind of relationship that could last.

I had good memories of my father from the first years of my life. My daddy was a drop-dead gorgeous man, who many women drooled over. They couldn't have him, because my mom had his heart.

My dad resembled Ron O'Neal—a quiet, thoughtful kind of handsome that gave him an air of mystery.

Once, my godmother didn't have a date to the prom. My mom allowed my dad to accompany my godmother, one "APB," to the prom as her date. She wanted to ensure that APB experienced one of the main highlights of being a senior in high school—dancing with a handsome, charming man.

I remembered my father being there, tucking me into bed at night after working long shifts at Greater Southeast Hospital. He hadn't yet become a truck driver—the job that would eventually take him away for weeks at a time.

My daddy was huge in my mind. He was literally huge, compared to my three-year-old self. I imagined that nothing could stop him. He could protect me from anything. And I knew, as he smiled down at me, that he would.

But then it all changed.

Full confession: I don't know exactly how or why. My parents never told me, and I never asked. I didn't want to hurt either of them, and they acted like porcupines when the question came up.

My mother said only this: that she'd never say anything bad about my daddy. My dad didn't say anything at all.

Maybe it was my mother's lifestyle. Maybe my dad, like Uncle Strap, couldn't bear the way she put herself and others in danger. Maybe he knew about the violence she did, the violence that could easily come back to haunt her. Maybe he couldn't give this family his all for that reason. Maybe it would have been too much for him to get too close, knowing of the danger.

Or maybe it was *his* lifestyle. His job as a trucker paid well—better than almost anything you could do legally without a college degree. But it meant that he was gone almost all the time, exhausted most of the time when he was home. He'd always lived far more on the road than with his family. Maybe at some point, having five percent of my father stopped being enough to satisfy Lady D.

It certainly wasn't enough to satisfy me.

After we moved into my grandpa's house, I saw my daddy maybe three times a year. For Christmas, Easter, and birthdays. He'd be there, smiling, with a big box of presents. But all I really wanted was *him*. And that was what he could not seem to understand, could not seem to give.

I ached when I went over to the neighbors' houses, to

my friends' houses, where they had two parents around. Even seeing my grandma and grandpa, two people who were so different but loved each other so much. A man and a woman who'd been loving each other, living together, for seventy years by the end.

I wanted my mother to have the way they looked at each other. I wanted to have my daddy there, like the neighbor kids did. To have your dad casually come out into the backyard and tell you it was time for dinner. To have him sitting, bored, at a parent-teacher conference. To be at a basketball game and know that he was there too. That was like magic to me.

I missed my daddy so much. I don't know if he ever knew.

Lord knows my mother was the queen of self-sufficiency. She refused to demand anything of him.

A couple of times a year, she'd get mad about her Bear missing her daddy and she'd call my dad, digging up whatever new phone number he had. In the era before cell phones, his trucker's life meant there was a real logistical problem with keeping track of him. It was a different hotel room, a different trucker's barracks, every week.

So it was maybe only twice a year that I'd get to hear his voice on the phone between holidays. Get to listen to him, enthralled, and pour my heart out to him, him never knowing how I treasured the sound of his voice. I didn't have words to say it. What child does?

My mother never asked him for child support. Never

tried to take him to court, never tried to make him do anything. Whatever choice they'd both made, she respected it.

And why would she need a man? She was herself a high-end breadwinner and a consummate parent. If that hadn't been clear before, it became so the moment my Bernard came into the world.

Lady D was so proud of her grandchild. And yet, somehow, just the right amount.

We'd argue sometimes over how to parent him. And in hindsight, my mother was always right. I was seventeen and she was, somehow, far wiser than anyone expected.

My mother would watch Bernard with glee—sometimes we fought over who *got* to watch him, to be with him for the day. Although I was still in high school for the first year of his life—my mother wouldn't hear of me dropping out—he was well cared for by an abundance of grandparents, great-grandparents, and great-aunts.

Lady D would parade my Bernard up and down the street, up and down the neighborhood.

"Look at him," she'd say to friends, neighbors, to anyone who walked by. "Isn't this the prettiest baby you have ever seen?"

Bernard would wave his tiny hands and gurgle happily in her arms.

And yet, she never let me forget my responsibility to him. She never let me off easy.

If I was going out with friends, she'd agree to watch him—but only after I'd bathed him, fed him, and put him to sleep. She refused to do these things in my place. She refused to let me forget that I was his mother, that any baby I gave birth to was mine to raise.

She took parental responsibility seriously, as she always did. And I think she felt the same about Bernard as she felt about me. That a mother couldn't give her all to more than one child.

And so she'd be Bernard's everything, give him everything she could. But she discouraged me from having any more babies.

"Bear," she'd say, "you've got to give this one your all."

I took Bernard to playdates with his half-brother, for a while. It was difficult and awkward, me and another poor girl staring at each other over our baby sons. Easier, probably, because their father was in prison. Easier because we had already realized that B.J. would be no worthy partner for us, no father to these boys, even if the other woman had not existed.

But it was still too hard. Over time, we grew apart. The playdates stopped. B.J.'s boys still know each other to this day—but they are not close. There has always been something of a tension between them. Something of a resentment—not of each other, but of the father who left them both for the fast life.

I know the pain of missing a father well. Of wondering why he isn't there for you, why he doesn't want to be. And so, I could not believe my luck when Marquis came into our lives while Bernard was still a baby.

I was parked at a stoplight the first time I spoke to him. He was in the next car over. He rolled down his window to talk to me—this man who looked handsome, strong, and wholesome. This man who looked like he'd walked right out of some happily-ever-after romance movie.

I'd made no serious attempts at dating—or at least, had no serious luck—since leaving B.J. and giving birth to Bernard. Most men steered clear of a woman with a little one who was not his. Especially a woman who was so young.

The stigma of the unwed teenage mother was even stronger in the 90s than it is today. That I was still in high school, that I planned to go to college, didn't matter to anyone.

If anything, that made some men run further away. "She's got a kid, *and* she's responsible?" The worst possible combination for a teenaged or twenty-something playboy.

So I'd learned what I had to do when men flirted with me, as Marquis clearly was. As he chatted me up, asked me what such a pretty lady was doing driving alone, I scooched back so that he could see the passenger seat.

"I'm not alone," I said. "Marquis, meet my son."

Bernard, God bless him, was just learning to talk. But he'd always been naturally charismatic. He strained in his car seat, sat up as straight as he could to try to look taller. To try to look like a big boy. And he waved with his chubby fingers.

To my shock, Marquis smiled. His face lit up. He looked like he was in love. And he wasn't looking at me. He was in love with my little baby.

And right then, I felt my own heart start to flutter. Who was this wonderful man, and where had he come from?

Marquis, Bernard, and I had lunch together that day. Marquis paid. It was clear that he wasn't *just* interested in me: far from it.

And as I watched this new man in my life play with Bernard like he was his very own daddy, my heart began to soar.

Maybe Bernard would get a good father after all.

$$$

Marquis and I didn't move too fast. By nineteen, I had learned to be wary. But I had also learned other things, and he surprised me by un-teaching those things at every turn.

From B.J., I had learned that love means jealousy. I'd learned that when a man was interested in me, when he said I was beautiful, when he brought me flowers, it meant that he would soon start demanding things of me. He would want to know where I was at all times. He would want sex. He would demand explanations if I went out with friends, or if I didn't pick up my phone.

Marquis surprised me by doing none of these things. He surprised me by expressing unwavering *support.*

He spent time with me and Bernard because he *wanted* to—not because he figured that meant I would owe him. He appreciated me as a woman, but he treated me like a *person.* Like an equal. Like his sister.

My success mattered to him more than me doing what he wanted. In fact, all he seemed to *want* was for me to succeed.

I began to revise my ideas about what was possible. His behavior was so *different* from B.J.'s—the behavior B.J. had always insisted was *normal,* inevitable, the cost of being in love—that it made me reevaluate everything.

With B.J., I had *imagined* him attending my son's parent-teacher conferences, his basketball games. I had *imagined* him as the supportive dad he *could* be. I had taken it upon myself to try to change him into that, or simply to hope.

I was taking two years off of school, wanting to be there for Bernard in his most vulnerable, formative years. My mother had agreed to this, but had *no* plans to let me off the hook for college entirely. And as we sat around my grandma's kitchen table, Bernard in my mother's lap and Marquis sitting next to me, he agreed that that was absolutely right.

I *would* go back to college, he said. I was too smart not to. And he'd support me in becoming anything I wanted to become. He'd get transferred to a closer airport.

At the time, he worked as a mechanic for the major airlines, and his home base was more than sixty miles away. But he'd do whatever he had to do, in terms of money or time, to make sure that I got that degree and Bernard got the best of everything.

Sitting across the table, my mother smiled. Still Lady D, she did not look a single inch a grandma. Her skin seemed to defy aging—maybe because of the hours she spent each day caring for it. She was still resplendent, sexual, alive.

But she sat across from me, bouncing her only grandchild in her lap, and she smiled. The kind of smile she got when a plan was coming together. The kind of smile she got that told me I was doing very, very well.

My heart sang. I was on the way, finally, I told myself. I'd thought that B.J. was the one, but no. This man, this wonderful man, would be my child's father. And my mother would grow old slowly, along with us, and maybe move into our house someday.

We'd create a whole new home base—a home not cursed by the deaths of my grandfather and my Uncle Kool Breeze, by the violence of Uncle Strap and the violations of cousin Bigelow.

We'd create a place untainted by fear, untainted by violence, and it would be to this home that Bernard brought his friends and, someday, his lovers. He would have two loving parents and his loving grandmother, Lady D.

Marquis and I had been together for a year when

he formally introduced me to his mother. She beckoned Bernard—who was now old enough to toddle to her and try to crawl into her lap. As he looked up at her, bright-eyed and curious, she bent to kiss his curly hair.

"This is my grandbaby," said this woman who I had just met. "And he always will be."

I watched with giddy astonishment.

Lady D was enough grandparent for any child, all on her own. But it couldn't hurt for him to have more family. You can never have too much family.

On Christmas that year, I saw Marquis's whole big, happy family, opening up their arms to my baby. And to me. I couldn't believe it.

It seemed like our perfect future was finally in the pipes. It seemed like nothing could go wrong.

8

THE GODMOTHER

Unknown to me, as I slept peacefully in my new house with my loving boyfriend and my precious baby boy, something dark was brewing in my mother's world.

No one knows exactly what my mother knew, or when she knew it. The only clue we have is this:

My cousin Killa, my mother's partner in crime since before I was born, had continued to work closely with her as the years passed. He'd become an expert hustler under the tutelage of Lady D. So much so that he'd recently decided to strike out on his own.

He'd begun procuring raw product from his own supplier and running his own supply chain. In doing so, he'd moved from being one of Lady D's subsidiaries, a part of her network of profits, to becoming her competition.

My mother was upset about this. It was as much the principle of the thing as it was the profits. Why had my cousin chosen to separate himself from her?

My mother was never hurting for money or influence. Killa was no threat to her. But he *was* family, a nephew who she'd often treated like a son.

His choice to go independent, then, was not just a matter of economic competition: it was as though he were rejecting her leadership. Rejecting his status as a member of her family, his place under her wing.

She'd been upset. She'd questioned his wisdom, his ability to protect himself now that he was out from under her umbrella. She had worried about him. She'd been indignant that he'd make this move without consulting her.

For my cousin Killa's part, he wanted to grow. Deena's ambition and relentless desire for perfection had infected him, and he realized he'd grown as much as he could while staying with her. He hadn't consulted her because he'd been afraid—afraid that she'd react exactly as she did. Afraid she'd say he couldn't hack it on his own.

As a result, the two of them hadn't spoken in weeks. Until my mother called him up to meet with her one day, out of the blue.

Killa knew as soon as he entered the little diner that something was terribly wrong. My mother looked tired. Subdued. Almost haggard. She looked as though she'd aged a great deal, very quickly.

She looked *worried.*

This was particularly alarming because it *never* happened. Nobody in living memory had seen Lady D seriously question her own judgment or really *worry* about anything. Her passion for life was a raging inferno that could not be quenched, a blazing supernova that lit up the darkness around her.

Her confidence was so consistent—and so well-supported by her flawless track record of success—that it was as much a part of her as her high cheekbones.

Yet now, it seemed to be gone. She was acting strangely, and Killa was terrified.

"Are you okay?" he asked immediately, the recent squabble forgotten. He slid into the booth across from her and leaned forward in concern, wondering what could possibly affect his auntie so.

"Yeah, I'm fine." My mother waved her hand, unconvincingly trying to brush the concern off. "There's nothing to worry about. Don't worry. But I need to ask a favor of you."

That *almost* made Killa feel better. If my mother was asking favors, it meant she was getting things done. It meant she was handling business. He may have gone financially independent, but he, like everyone who knew my mother, was still eager to respond to her beck and call.

Lady D only organized things for the good of the family, and there was almost nobody who wouldn't do what she asked.

Then she told him what the favor was, and his stomach hit the floor.

"I need you to stay away from my place. Don't come around anymore. Can you do that for me?" she asked.

Killa's stomach churned. "Stay away? Why, auntie? What is going on?"

It was clear that everything was *not* okay. It was clear that the words weren't spoken in anger, or spite. This wasn't about hostility, or punishing him for leaving her operation. This was about protecting him.

Protecting him from what?

"Nothing's going on. Everything's fine. Just—" for maybe the first time ever, Lady D hesitated. "Just stay away from my place. Lay low. Can you do that?"

"What are you talking about? *Why?*"

And then my mother took a deep breath, knowing that she wouldn't get obedience if she didn't give an explanation.

"Because," she said, "if you come around and something happens to you, they'll never catch who did it."

It was the night before Thanksgiving, and Marquis and I were asleep in our bed. We weren't married yet—after my experience with B.J., I still had trouble believing that a good thing could last. But so far it had, and Marquis was a father to Bernard and a partner to me in every possible way. We had a house in Maryland, between Marquis's airport and my grandma's house.

And so I had gone to bed, warm and snug in Marquis's arms. Anticipating tomorrow, when we'd go to 4th Street to see my mother, my grandmother, and the whole extended family. All of the countless aunts and uncles and cousins still gathered there, in the home my grandparents had made, to pass countless soul food dishes with roots stretching back generations.

I was so anticipating that Thanksgiving dinner, and seeing my mother laugh as she held Bernard on her knee. It would be Marquis's first Thanksgiving with my family—my *whole* family in all of their wild, intimidating, uncontainable glory.

So I didn't know what to think when the phone rang at 2 a.m.

I pushed myself out of bed, drowsy. The landline on the bedside table was rattling and clanging, shattering the peace of the night. My first thought, as with an alarm clock, was just to shut it up.

I let my hand fall heavy on the receiver and pressed it to my face. I slurred a little, irritation in my voice, as I said: "Who is this?"

"Bear? Bear, is that you?"

My heart froze in my chest. It was my Aunt Gerri, my mother's sister. And I could hear in her voice that something was terribly wrong.

I swung my legs over the side of the bed, not sure what to do. From the adrenaline in her voice, the tears I could hear on the other end of the line, my body was screaming at me to do something. But what?

"Auntie, what's wrong?" I was already pulling my shoes on. I didn't know why. Aunt Gerri's home was forty-five minutes away by car, but somewhere in my mind, I was planning to bust in and save the day.

"Bear—Deena—she's—"

"She's *what*?" Hearing my mother's name sparked fire in my blood. The same kind of rage she had at the thought of somebody touching her Bear. I'd kill a nigga if that's what it took to keep my mother safe.

"Deena's *dead!*" Aunt Gerri screamed. Her tears and breath cracked, heavy, over the phone. "She's dead, Bear. Somebody killed her."

My blood ran hot and cold at once. I think I froze for a moment, with the receiver in hand. Some part of my brain rejected the news. It couldn't be true. It just couldn't be.

And yet, of course it could. My mother ran with gangsters. Her colleagues and her competition were a mob-like tangle of crime families, who would not hesitate to kill if they felt it necessary. Or even just if somebody wanted to.

It was this possibility that had driven Uncle Strap to violence. This possibility that had lurked in the back of my mind, hung over everyone's head, for years. Decades.

But it couldn't be true.

"Bear? Are you there? I said—I said, somebody killed your mother."

I got up and ran up and down the hall outside my bedroom several times. Screaming, hollering, crying. I made it to the front door and beat my fists against it.

Why? I couldn't do anything. But being in our front room felt like being in my grandma's front room, right in front of the kitchen where my mother held court. Beating against that door felt like beating against *their* door, the door to the house where I'd lived with my mother for the better part of twenty years.

The house where part of me still lived.

I stood there, banging on the door and screaming in disbelief. Not knowing what I could do. As that fact filtered down to me, slowly—that something had really happened, that I couldn't do anything here—I ran back to the bedroom, where the phone lay on the blankets I had flung aside.

Marquis was up now. He'd gotten out of bed and was staring at me with huge eyes. He approached slowly, his hands outstretched in caution. I could see that he wanted to comfort me. To hold me and help me through.

My breathing slowed a little. I wasn't ready to be held, but I wasn't completely alone, either.

"Chelley, what—" Marquis tried.

I snatched the phone up again.

"Who did it?" I demanded. "Who killed her."

"Well, Bear, if I knew *that* I wouldn't be talking to you." There was grief in my aunt's voice, but also a savage anger. I knew what she meant. If she knew who had killed my mother, she'd be out killing them back.

"There are detectives here," she said slowly, and I realized I could hear a little background noise behind her. Not the usual background noise for our house. Men. Black men with preppy college accents—talking in low voices. Strange echoes, as though the house were full of people and equipment. "They want to ask some questions. I can send them over there—"

"No," I answered sharply. I took my shoes off and began to shuck my pajamas. "I'm coming over there. I'll be there in—half an hour. Don't let them leave."

"Half an hour? Bear, it's..." I could almost hear Gerri look around the chaos that was my grandmother's house. Think the better of what she was about to say. These were not normal circumstances. Nothing would ever be normal again. "Okay," she said finally. "Okay. I'll be here."

By that time I was hopping on one leg, one leg in my pants and one leg out of it. Marquis was still watching, terror-stricken. He'd heard the words, "Who killed her?"

and that was all he knew.

"Chelley, what—" He tried again as I let the receiver drop to the floor.

"It's my mother," I said, tearing open the closet door and ripping a shirt off the hanger. "She's dead."

Marquis sat in the car, bless him, cradling a sleepy Bernard as I stomped up the front steps and into the apartment building where my mother had been living with her boyfriend for several months. The apartment building where she'd been killed.

The street and parking lot were filled with cop cars, blue and red lights flashing, with yellow tape. The scene was swarming with strangers, and their watchful eyes made the hair on the back of my neck stand up.

I knew something about these detectives. My mother had known something about these detectives. Working for an attorney and a distribution operation at the same time taught you a lot.

I knew that these detectives didn't close most of the cases that crossed their desks. I knew that half the time, when they did, they got the wrong guy.

And so I was on a prowl of my own around the property, looking for clues. Not in the footprints or fingerprints or blood spatter patterns, but in the ways the people were acting.

There are few strangers in the criminal underground, and no random acts of violence. It's almost always someone who knows the victim. Someone who dated or did business with her. And the perpetrators aren't stupid. They know they can't hide behind anonymity, so they don't try to hide. Instead, they come in close. To keep any witnesses quiet.

A small crowd had gathered around the apartment complex, despite the hour. Many had gathered around my grandmother's house and then made the sojourn to the apartment building when they heard it had been the scene of the crime.

A ring of shocked faces with big eyes stared at me, and at everybody who was inside the caution tape going up around the front lawn. Faces we knew. Friends, neighbors. Associates.

"Bear." Lisa, a woman from across the street, reached out with empty hands as I passed her. "Bear, what *happened*?" Lisa's eyes were all wonder and pain. She looked to me for answers. Or for tips, about who knew what.

"We don't know, Lisa." I was acting when I reached out to her, let her warm fingers curl around mine. But when my hands touched hers, I realized I was shaking. The adrenaline tearing through me was like nothing I'd ever known. My mind was operating separately from my body.

I looked around sharply, then, a thought striking me. "Lisa, where's the Boss?"

Lisa looked startled. Afraid. She glanced fearfully at the detectives who swarmed the scene. The Boss was her brother. He was also my mother's supplier and business partner.

"Why would he be..." I realized then that she thought that I suspected him. I *did*, but I didn't want her to know that.

"I'm not saying he was here, Lisa," I snapped. "I mean, where *is* he! There's nothing my mother was doing that the Boss wasn't in on. What if they got him too?"

Her eyes got huge, and she pulled away from me. She looked across the lawn, at the neighbors gathering, for a long moment.

Then she broke into a run back toward her car. She'd find a telephone and call her brother. Or, that's what she wanted me to think.

I watched her go with a sinking feeling in my stomach.

I had learned some things from my mother. Enough. Although I'd never played her game, I knew how it was done.

And I knew that I couldn't afford to be honest with anybody here. Not anymore. A sort of protective armor started to go up around my heart.

I couldn't trust any of them to be honest with me, either.

The realization broke through me in waves. My

mother had taught me how to do everything. Everything, but live without her.

My whole life, she'd been close. Always there when I needed her. She'd been my rock. My confidante. Now she was gone, and my world was empty.

There were hours and days when I broke down just like she had when her daddy died. I lay on the couch in my and Marquis's house, keening and crying while he rubbed my back and tried to do something, anything to help. Nothing would help.

Well. One thing helped.

One thing got me off the couch, focused and yet numb, in a sort of warrior mode that existed separate from reality. In one pursuit, I could pretend my mother was waiting for me on the other end. That she'd come back if I could just solve the mystery.

The mystery of who had killed her.

I didn't trust the detectives any more than my mother would have. I trusted the neighbors even less. I'd seen enough of the world she lived in—the neighborly intimacy of violence, the speed with which one could become the other.

Dealers were usually killed by their rivals. By people from other territories, trying to expand their turf. By people they'd offended, insulted, lashed out against.

Usually.

But sometimes, it was their suppliers. Sometimes it was their business partners. Sometimes it was someone incredibly close, someone in the crime family who decided that one member had become a weak link or an obstacle to personal ambition.

It could have been a rival or a friend, then. It could have been an enemy or a compatriot. It could have been anyone.

One day passed after my mother's murder. Two. Three. Three long days of sitting alone in my own front room, or at a chair around my mother's kitchen table, shuffling back and forth to cope as best I could.

All while collecting information, without anyone quite realizing I was doing it.

Neighbors came out of the woodwork. Everyone was full of questions.

Who had been angry with Lady D? Who had been fighting with her? Who would have had a reason?

Names were traded, tossed back and forth. Names of people from all around the city.

But nobody died. None of those people who were spoken about turned up dead or missing. There were no more mysterious shootings, no triumphant entrances into the back door of my grandma's house by someone claiming to have shot my mother's killer.

And that was how I knew that it was one of her friends. One of those who had gathered around the table with my mother, night after night, laughing and joking and talking shop.

If they hadn't killed anybody yet, it meant they knew who was guilty. And that it wasn't an enemy or a rival. It was a friend—a member of their own operation. My mother's enforcers knew who had killed her, and were fine with it.

The people I grew up with had sanctioned my mother's murder. Maybe one of the neighbors had even pulled the trigger themselves.

I was certain of this by the time her funeral came. As friends and family, neighbors—extended family, as far as we were concerned—gathered to carry her casket, I was sure the killer was there. Maybe he was helping to carry the casket. Maybe she was serving fruit salad at the dessert table.

I knew that it was probably the person with the most visible concern, the most tragedy in their face, the most prying eyes and questions. And right now, that meant the Boss and his sister.

The Boss stuck close to me. He was a short man who made up for his small stature with a big personality, big charm, and a big ego. He wasn't the neatest or most stylish of men, but his smile and his voice were hard to miss. If only because of his way of sweeping in, taking center stage, channeling all attention toward himself.

He came around every time I was at my grandparents' house, which became the focal point of mourning. In that neighborhood, my mother had been like a celebrity. It was where all of her most intimate contacts lived, from her childhood friends to her business acquaintances. Her death wasn't just a family affair: it rocked the whole community.

People got shot for selling drugs all the time. But Lady D, who everyone loved? Never Lady D.

The Boss visited daily, trying to stick close to me. He wanted to know what I knew, who I suspected, what I was doing about the investigation. He had his sisters bring over cake. He tried to convince me that he knew who had killed my mother.

And of course, his story was that it wasn't him.

I'd always hated that nickname of his. 'The Boss' was no older than me—in fact, he had been the neighbor boy, one of my classmates growing up. We might as well have been cousins. Except that I had never liked him. He thought too fast, moved too fast, turned up in all the wrong places at the wrong times.

It was my mother who had started calling him "Boss" after he climbed his way to the top of the distribution ladder with alarming speed. She'd known how to flatter and stroke an ego, how to make a young man like her. By deferring to him. By making it clear that she was his loyal servant.

I'd always hated their relationship. The way she'd all but bow down to him, stroking his ego for her own ends. Maybe stroking it a little too much. The way he got so full of himself so fast. The way he looked at me, looked down on me, like somebody he'd surpassed.

Nobody got under my skin more than the neighbor boy who became the Boss to my mother. And now he was all over me.

"Bear." He slunk in through the backdoor of my grandmother's house after the funeral. After helping to carry the casket, a dark wooden coffin, and lay it in a hole in the ground.

I'd fought the impulse to crawl in after her and let them cover me with dirt. My mother had been my whole world, the only constant in my life. Only Bernard, looking up at me with his bright little eyes as Marquis held him, sparked anything like life in my soul.

Helping to carry the casket. Laying my mother to rest. Coming in through the back door to sit at her now-empty table. These were things that any neighbor, any family member would have done.

But there was something clandestine in his eyes, in his movements, as he beckoned me to my mother's kitchen table. As he leaned forward, beckoning me to come closer.

Her absence hurt like an open wound, as did the silence in the kitchen. Everybody was a little afraid to trespass on my mother's domain. As though if we avoided the place, pretended she was still in there, she would be. As though if we didn't look at the empty table, it wouldn't be empty.

Now the Boss was hunkering down in a chair across

that table, the same place he used to sit while he and my mother talked strategy.

I knew danger when I saw it, but I also knew opportunity. So I approached him stiffly, pulling a chair out and sitting too straight-backed and proud in what had once been my mother's seat.

"Bear," he said again. "They've got Hunter at one of the hospitals around here."

I stared levelly at the man who was acting like he'd given me new information. I knew—everybody in my mother's family knew—that my mother's boyfriend had been with her when she was shot.

The truth was that no one, including my family, liked Hunter as a partner for my mom. He was loud, boisterous, and talked too much. He was what the streets would deem "hot."

That meant he bought down unnecessary heat, or attention from the cops and the competition. Loudness, talkativity, an inability to restrain one's mouth—those were the kinds of traits that would get you killed in my mother's world.

My mother's family and colleagues had accepted Hunter because of their respect for my mom. But everyone, including my family, blamed Hunter at least somewhat for my mom's death.

He'd taken several bullets too, and been left for dead. Many people in the family believed that he had been the real target for the hit, and that Lady D's closeness to him had made her collateral damage.

Hunter had almost died. But he'd survived. Lived, maybe, to tell what really happened. He'd been barely breathing when the cops arrived. Now, he was in a hospital room upstate under the name of John Doe.

John Doe. Anonymous. In case the person who had shot him came to finish the job.

"They've got Hunter upstate, and Bear—I'm pretty sure it was him. I'm pretty sure he's the one who shot your mother."

My eyes grew wide. My blood ran cold. I wanted to believe it was a lie, that my simple picture of the world was true. That this man—the Boss, who I had always resented for thinking himself above me, was the culprit. Or at least in league with them.

But I also wanted, very badly, to have closure. And blaming the Boss had its own complications. It was easy to despise him, to suspect him. But if he had done it, and no one had taken him out already—that meant many other people were complicit. Beloved friends, neighbors, family. If he had done it and none of them had struck out at him, it meant many people I loved were guilty too.

So there was an appeal in what he was suggesting. In believing that it was a near stranger to me, my mother's most recent boyfriend, who had killed her. That would absolve so many people. If only it were true.

The first objection was obvious: "Why the Hell would Hunter kill my mother, then shoot himself too?" I demanded, my arms still crossed. "He loved her. He would never kill her." For all the reservations I had about Hunter, I *did* believe he loved my mother.

"Besides," I pointed out, "this wasn't a flesh wound. He barely survived. They say he wouldn't have lived much longer if the cops had shown up later. You don't do that to yourself, just to cover your own tracks."

The Boss leaned in close, conspiratorial. "*Exactly*," he whispered.

Almost against my will, I leaned in toward him and narrowed my eyes in fierce suspicion.

"Nobody's gonna look at him while he's lying up at the hospital half-dead," the Boss whispered. "They'd accuse Al Capone before they'd accuse the other victim. I'll bet the detectives aren't even looking at him—and neither are any of us. Why do you think we haven't found who did it yet?"

It was a seductive line of reasoning. That no one had been killed, not because it was my mother's own people who had done it, but because the real culprit was upstate at the hospital under an anonymous name. That it had been a love affair gone wrong—not a result of my mother's own dangerous choices.

"How sure are you about this?" I asked the Boss, probing his eyes with my own.

The look on his face chilled me to the bone. His eyes

glinted in that way I'd never been able to read. That way that said he knew *something*, something secret.

But what did he know? And as his eyebrows furrowed into a frown, I saw a shadow. A shadow of the rage I felt over my mother's death.

"I'm dead sure, Bear," he said. "Dead sure."

9

THE BOSS

Precious few people were allowed to see Hunter. The hospital was afraid that whoever had tried to kill him would sneak in and finish the job. So it was only intimate family members who were even allowed to know where he was.

Lady D's family was allowed to know. And that included me.

I prayed, as Andrea Prince and I drove with the Boss in the passenger seat, that we were doing the right thing. My heart was pounding with excitement and terror.

Andrea Prince and I had ridden around with Boss for days, watching each other's backs. We felt uneasy and uncertain of the concocted, lying-ass story he was trying to sell us. We just felt that lil' bitch-ass coward nigga Boss was lying. It seemed to us that his ass was definitely in on it, and that he had something to hide.

And yet, we had to investigate.

What if it really was Hunter who had murdered my mother? What if that was why the detectives I spoke to said they had no leads? What if Hunter, with his blabbermouth personality, had had something to do with her death?

And yet. What if Hunter really was an innocent victim? What if it was the Boss who'd pulled the trigger, as we suspected?

It was difficult to think clearly while friends and neighbors swirled around, asking questions and proposing suspects.

It was difficult to think clearly when the detectives who I called daily told me that they had no firm leads, and spoke about my mother like she was just another drug dealer. A statistic.

So here I was, my knuckles white on the steering wheel as I navigated my car through traffic with a man I despised sitting beside me.

I hated the way the Boss watched me as I drove. How could he be so calm? There was something off about his behavior—about the way he acted like it was his job to find my mother's killer, but didn't seem that broken up about her death. He'd been solemn-faced at the funeral, eyes downcast. But no more than that. I had yet to see him weeping.

And yet, who could feel my mother's death like I could? Who except her daughter could be expected to cry and cry, inconsolably, in her car in the church parking lot? Was I expecting too much of the Boss, of the others? Could any of them meet my standards of grief?

My hand shook as I put the car into park and stared up at the huge, square building of the hospital. It was such a pedestrian sight. I'd passed hospitals like this every day of my adult life, on my way to work and school. Yet now it was a strange and terrifying place.

Now it held the only living soul who had been there when my mother died.

I smiled politely at the front desk staff as I led the Boss into the building. I was dressed to the nines. Overdressed, probably. But anxiety made me compensate. I was here, in a way, representing my mother. I wanted to look as sharp and official as she had always looked when she wore her investigator's suit.

We rode the elevator to Hunter's floor in agonizing silence. I looked at my shoes, at the mirror-shiny ceiling, at the small cracks in the floor tiles. Anywhere but at the man I'd grown up with. The man who could now either be my mother's killer, or her avenger.

The walk down the final hallway seemed to take forever. At last, we stood outside of Hunter's room. The blinds were drawn in the window between his room and the door. I glanced both ways to make sure no nurses or security staff were watching, and then I turned the old steel doorknob.

Hunter was lying in a bed, covered in white sheets. The man was the spitting image of Idris Elba, except for the bandages and the tubes that ran out of his body to connect to various bags and beeping monitors around him. His eyes opened sleepily at first. He probably thought it was a nurse who had opened the door.

He saw me and started to smile.

Then he saw the Boss behind me, and his eyes grew huge.

My pulse quickened.

Does he know?

I felt certain that the man who had murdered my mother was in this small room with us. But which man was it? The detectives were useless, so it was on me to find out. How could I be sure?

The Boss smiled big when he saw Hunter. He moved up from behind me, walking slowly toward the hospital bed.

"Hey, Hunter," he said.

Hunter seemed to be shrinking back into his pillows. I heard the beeps on his heart rate monitor speed up. I wanted to get between them. But I couldn't. Seeing the way the two men looked at each other, I was paralyzed.

Is he scared of the Boss? Or scared of being found out?

"It's good to see you're feeling better, man," the Boss said, all friendly. "We were all really scared. The same thing could have happened to you that happened to Lady D. Couldn't it?"

Hunter was squirming like he'd squirm right out of the bed if he could. He stared at the Boss in sheer terror. The beeps on his heart monitor were still speeding up.

Andrea and I could see how upset Hunter was getting. We could see that it wasn't the kind of upset that came from someone lying about you, or even from fear of going to jail.

It was the kind of fear you felt when you stared down your killer.

Hunter was sure that the Boss was there to kill and silence him. And in that moment, I was sure of it too.

"What the hell is going on!" Andrea demanded, speaking up. She took a step closer to the Boss. "Something isn't right, Boss. Why is he so upset?"

The Boss ignored her. "What happened, nigga?" the Boss demanded of Hunter. Meanness and venom dripped from his voice. "The streets are talking. Word on the street is, you're telling people Slim had something to do with the hit on Lady D."

Slim. The Boss's closest business partner, outside of my mother. The Boss's partner in crime. If the Boss was the muscle, the executor, Slim was the brains of their operation.

The Boss leaned in closer to Hunter. Hunter tried to sit up angrily, glaring at the Boss with bared teeth.

"I didn't say y'all called the hit," he spat. "I said it might have been them niggas from uptown. This is some bullshit. You come here blaming me for something I didn't do."

"Don't be putting Slim's name out there," the Boss hissed, getting close to Hunter's face. "Because if it had been Slim, you would be dead too."

That was when I knew, watching the two men together. The way the Boss loomed over Hunter with menace in his face. His hands in his pockets, as if he had a gun with a silencer on him.

The hospital had no metal detectors. And Hunter was the only witness to my mother's murder. His heart was racing even faster than mine, the monitor giving an almost continuous *beeeep.*

I opened my mouth to scream at the exact moment that a nurse opened the hospital room door.

"What is going on here? You all are not supposed to be here!" She knew a serious situation when she saw one. "I am calling the police *now,*" she declared, and stormed out of the room to the nurse's station.

It was a clever move: as long as she was in the hallway, there were lots of witnesses to anything that might happen to her. The Boss might have pulled the trigger on all three of us while we were alone, but now he'd been seen. And he knew better than to make more witnesses.

As soon as she was gone, the Boss, Andrea Prince, and I ran.

An awful, bad feeling had settled in me like none I'd known before. I knew we'd come close to witnessing the Boss kill Hunter—and it would have been all my fault if he'd gotten to finish the deed.

I knew now that I should have spoken up more. I should have trusted my instincts. I'd known I couldn't trust that man, so why had I done it? If he'd blown Hunter away, it would have been on my conscience forever.

My face burned with shame. My heart pounded with fear. What had I done? What had almost happened here?

The only thing that saved us was the Boss's sense of self-preservation. He had just enough sense to back out of a plan when people he couldn't eliminate got involved.

Well. Now I knew. After watching the Boss stand over Hunter with a look that said he was ready to kill, there was no longer any doubt in my mind.

I knew who had killed my mother.

They found my mother's body half inside of her apartment building, half outside on the front walk.

Seeing the photos of the scene was heartbreaking. It was an experience I'll never get over. I replay the scenes over and over in my mind, imagining my mother's final moments.

There was my mother, just as I'd always known her. The impeccable skin and hair and body, impeccable sense of style. She'd fallen, seemingly, at the precise moment that she opened the door to her home.

She had multiple gunshot wounds. Some entered through her back and exited through her chest. The one that had killed her, the coroner thought, entered through her back and exited through her skull.

Had she been running, I wondered? Running down the walkway of her apartment building at night, sprinting toward shelter? Did she know she was being chased?

Or had she been taken by surprise? Gunned down during the ordinary, pedestrian act of entering her apartment building?

And *why?*

I knew from conversations with my mother that she was ready to get out of the drug game. She was tired. The streets were hot. Slim and some of her other associates were being investigated on charges of organized crime. She didn't want any part of it.

People in her network had been dropping like flies for months. Some were locked up, while others were murdered on suspicion of "snitching" or as a preventative safety measure against it. With people going down left and right, the D.C. streets just weren't safe. And so, finally, Lady D had decided that she wanted out.

I hadn't thought too much of it—someone was always going to jail in the drug game. The most remarkable thing had been that Lady D was talking about getting out. That should have been a red flag. But I never thought to doubt that my mother could do it safely. She always did what she said she would, and she never got into anything she couldn't get out of.

It was possible that someone believed my mother had snitched, or had feared that she might as the heat turned up.

I knew otherwise. She'd told me, in the kind of solemn, private mother-daughter talk where she never lied:

"I'd die before I'd snitch, Bear." She'd beat this into my head, gesturing with her perfectly manicured hands.

"If someone takes out one of my people, you best believe Imma handle that shit. We take care of our own. If someone stabs one of my people, they gon' get this ice pick in them. But I will never snitch."

I knew that was true. But I didn't know if the Boss believed it. Or if he cared. To him, casting suspicion on my mother might have been just what he needed to eliminate a powerful, more experienced rival.

When the cops started to come around, tempers ran high. Grudges and competition turned into paranoia. Allegations of snitching could be used as an excuse to eliminate any rivals, personal or professional. My mother had always played a clean game, but you didn't move in that life without knowing how these things are done. Without seeing them happen.

Everyone knew that you rarely lived past forty if you played this game. But my mother had always been one of the smart ones. One of the lucky ones. One of the beloved ones.

She knew how to play politics, how to give other people enough of a cut and enough respect to satisfy them. She knew how far was too far, and how to play her cards just right.

Everyone who knew my mother loved her. Her exuberant joy. Her warmth. Her beauty.

Or so we'd thought.

Had she become a rival to someone, a power big enough that someone had decided she was a threat and she needed to be taken out?

Had she become a suspect in the "heat" on her operation? Had someone suspected her of snitching?

Or was it simply, always, inevitable? There was a reason why the average life expectancy for people in the game was thirty. But we'd always thought my mother would find her way out in peace.

I knew one thing for sure: my mother was *not* a snitch. Her relationship with law enforcement was love-hate—she used her knowledge of the law to *prevent* prosecutions.

She was a firm believer in the code of the street. If justice needed to be done, she handled it herself. Sometimes in a brutal fashion. But she would never, *ever* snitch.

Anyone who knew my mother would have known that she didn't snitch. That she didn't crack under pressure, no matter how much. But that didn't mean someone hadn't used the heat on her operation as an excuse to take her out.

And I had a pretty good idea of who it was. The Boss's grin haunted me for weeks as I tried to pick up the pieces of my life.

Going on without my mother was inconceivable. She was the one force, the one constant, who had always been there for me. She'd been there through the comings and goings of my father, my uncles, my B.J. She'd been there for the first steps of my tremulous, still-new relationship with Marquis. And she had promised me she'd never leave.

"You better believe I'll be there for Bernard's graduation. You better believe I'll always be there for you. You two are the most important things in my life, Bear. I've got your back."

This was the first promise to me that my mother had ever broken.

At home, I lay in bed, with no motivation to move. Bernard could sometimes rouse me, his bright eyes and small hands sparking life in my heart. Because of him, I knew I had to go on. But as soon as we were separated, I fell apart.

When I tried to go out to work or school, I'd sit in my

car crying. Screaming, really. Fists pounding the steering wheel.

How could my mother leave me?

Who would take care of me now, when no one else had had my back like she did?

How could I be here alone?

There was one thing, and only one thing, other than Bernard that motivated me. The fact that the detectives, in all their usual mediocrity, still hadn't figured out who killed her.

I had, but I couldn't prove it.

It wasn't surprising that the detectives had trouble. No one in the neighborhood would talk to them—especially in the first days after the killing. *Everyone* knew that her killers were close. Everyone knew that anyone who was even suspected of speaking with the cops could end up dead in an abandoned house with boards nailed over the windows.

I did not even share my suspicions, my certainty about the Boss, my experience with him in the hospital, with my family.

The Boss and his sister lived across the street from my grandmother's house. They still visited at least weekly, pretending to share condolences and remorse. They had fake conversations with my family, pretending to want to help with small projects around the house.

All the while, I knew that they were fishing for information. Who knew what, and would they talk? What would happen to any member of my family if they let something slip?

The Boss himself was often to be found, wearing a sad face, sitting at my mother's kitchen table or on the couch where she had grieved her father's passing. If it wasn't him, it was his sister: big-eyed Lisa who hounded me, almost followed me around, seemingly out of concern.

"Bear,"—she'd catch me in the church parking lot, her hands all clasped in grief—"this must be so hard for you. Why don't you come over? I'll cook dinner, and we can talk about it. You need someone to take care of you."

I hoped my smile was convincing. "Thank you so much for thinking of me during this time," I'd say. "But I have a baby boy to get back to."

I'd rush to my car then, hurry to slam the door shut and lock it. I'd pull out of the church parking lot as fast as I could, heart pounding.

I knew that just a few feet away from where I'd parked, Lisa's car waited. Full of family members, including the Boss. Eager to take me back to their place. Or maybe somewhere else.

10

THE INVESTIGATION

As the weeks passed, the heat on the neighborhood began to die down. The detectives from the local police department conducted their rounds with no more than routine enthusiasm.

The detectives were outsiders, trained in a distant school of criminal investigation and employed by a distant mayor who was not well-loved in the neighborhood.

I'm sure it didn't take long to become jaded in that profession. When people are dropping left and right and no one will talk to you or give you useful information, it must be easy to feel that the community doesn't *want* the killers to be found.

To these men, my mother was just another dead drug dealer. People in her profession were killed in the city on an at-least weekly basis.

In reality, she was the victim of a heinous crime. They didn't know my mother well enough to understand how extraordinary she was. How well-loved she was. How beautiful she was. How people got shot, but never Lady D.

I spoke to them, begged, pleaded, tried to make them understand. But I was her daughter—not an objective witness to the facts, as far as they were concerned.

Throughout the neighborhood, the only people who *would* talk to the cops were people who knew nothing, even if they thought they did. People who didn't know the rules of the game or its players.

Anyone within several degrees of separation from my mother refused to talk. They didn't want to be next.

As the detective's presence in the neighborhood waned—and the vigilance of the Boss's crew along with it—I knew it was time to conduct an investigation of my own.

I sat in my car in the parking lot of my mother's apartment building for a long time. My heart was pounding.

I *wanted* revenge. I wanted justice for my mom. I wanted to know with certainty who the hell killed my mom, and why!

But I also hated what I was about to do. There were dangers for me, my son, and my family.

Finally, I slammed the car door behind me and

walked up the narrow cement path to the doorway where my mother had died. I opened the door and stepped over the same doorway where my mother's dead, limp body had lain, shot up with bullet holes months before.

I was so scared, wondering what her last moments were like.

What were her last thoughts? I even wondered if that bitch-ass Boss and his crew were lying in wait here, waiting to kill me before I talked.

My mother and Hunter had lived on the third floor of this building. My mother had died on the first floor. Between here and there, someone must have seen something.

I paused and gathered myself in front of the first apartment door on the first-floor hallway. The door closest to where my mother had died. I was wearing my work clothes, a suit. I had wanted to look respectable. But now I wondered if that was the right choice.

I straightened my suit, took a deep breath, and knocked.

Nothing.

I let thirty seconds go by. Still nothing. I knocked again, rapping harder with my knuckles.

Nothing. Then a rustle. A pause. Footsteps.

The door creaked as it opened just a few inches. A man in a T-shirt stood inside. He looked at me with one eye through the door and started to close it again.

"Wait," I tried, and my voice came out sounding more desperate than I'd planned. "I'm Deena's daughter. The woman who was killed here a few weeks ago. Can I talk to you, please?"

Another pause. The man twisted to look behind him, back into his apartment. He hesitated.

"Please. I need to know if anyone saw anything. I need to know how my mother died."

For a minute, he didn't move.

"Please," I broke down, my chest aching. "I'm begging you. If you know anything or you heard anything, please tell me. Put yourself in my shoes. I'm a young mom myself, with a new baby. Trying to pick up the pieces of my life, and trying to determine what the future holds. I can't do that without help. Can you please help me? Please talk to me. I'm all alone in this world without a mother, and I need some help."

Please help me. It was a phrase I'd say many times as I haunted the hallways of my mother's last home, looking for information. Many people there lived by the code of the streets, and wouldn't talk to the police themselves. But it was hard to ignore a daughter's pleas for justice for her mother.

The door opened the rest of the way. The man was still looking behind him, but he waved me inside. "Okay, no problem," he said. "Come in. Have a glass of water, at least."

I was already shaking. I walked carefully over the stained carpet, into an unkempt living room where a woman was sitting on the couch. A soap opera was playing on TV.

The woman looked up sharply. "Black, who's this?" Her eyes were on her husband, not on me. Waiting for an explanation.

"I'm—the daughter of the woman who was shot outside your door." Now it was my turn to glance behind me. The door to the hallway had safely closed behind us. "I—the detectives can't find anything. No one will talk to them. I want some answers."

The woman's look of mistrust slowly softened as she looked me up and down. Saw that I was devastated and a mess underneath this suit. Not some arrogant, uninterested investigator.

"Oh, okay. No problem, sweetie. Sit down. You look very nice. I love that suit."

"Thank you. I work in a corporate office," I said apologetically. "I didn't mean to disturb you. I just—I need to know."

Black was coming back from the kitchen with a glass of water in each hand. "We saw a man," he said. "A little guy. Short. I thought he was a visitor, but then..." Black hesitated and looked at the woman.

"He held the doors closed." The words came out of

her mouth harsh, like she was angry at remembering it. “We couldn’t figure out what he was doing. We heard this commotion and we looked out of our peephole. This short guy was standing by the door, and he was holding it closed. This woman was trying to get in, yelling and pulling on the door.”

My blood froze. The image was all too vivid. My mother is running. Knowing, somehow, that they had decided to kill her. Running for her life, trying to seek shelter in her building.

Boss’s coward ass fit the description for sure. A short man. I imagined him standing by the door, making sure she couldn’t escape. Holding the door shut as my mother ran and tried desperately to open it.

On the outside, I had gone very still. The glass of water sat, untouched, in my hand. Condensation trickled down the side.

“The short man—what was his hair like?”

“Cornrows,” Black replied. “A little messy. They weren’t done by a beautician, that’s for sure. More like by a guy in a hurry.”

The Boss had been wearing loose, uneven cornrows when he came by my grandmother’s house the day after my mother’s murder. He’d never given his appearance as much care as my mother had given hers.

I had a sudden, vivid flashback to her sitting at our kitchen table, tinting her lashes.

"Thank you," I heard my own voice say. "Thank you so much. That sounds like somebody I know."

There are no words to describe the silence that descended. It's a uniquely awful thing. When you're with near-strangers and everybody knows that someone killed your mother. Everyone knows it was somebody you *know,* and everyone knows you're not gonna tell the police about it.

"Baby," the woman said gently, "you're not thinking about taking this into your own hands, are you?"

The thought flashed through my mind. *That bitch-ass Boss is gon' pay. I'm gon' make his ass suffer.* An eye for an eye.

But no. That was my mother's world. That was the place she had never wanted me to follow. I had to be there for Bernard. I couldn't risk incarceration.

And besides—I was sure that my mother was not his only victim. Watching how the Boss had stood over Hunter, the total ease with which he sat in my grandmother's kitchen, I was certain he had done this before. Many times.

The Boss would get his day in court. I was going to make sure of it.

"Detective Greene?"

There was a pause on the other end of the line. I could

almost hear the detective's crisp suit crinkling as I sat on the edge of the bed I shared with Marquis, my palms sweating.

"Miss Roy," he said finally. "I guess you're calling about your mother."

"Yes. I—"

"Well, you're talking to the wrong person, Miss Roy. I've been taken off the case."

My stomach dropped. How could the police department even think about closing my mother's case so soon?

I knew that no one had been willing to talk to them—that was not surprising. But surely they had to keep trying. That was their job. And what would I do if they did give up, if they did close the case, without bringing anyone to justice?

My head spun. "But Detective, I talked to someone who—"

"You're going to want to tell Agent Segal. This case has been taken over by the FBI. The safe streets task force, to be exact. They specialize in organized crime. They've been investigating a 'Murder for Hire' drug cartel in the area for years, and they think your mother's death was part of it. They've got surveillance, wiretaps, and more."

There was a new kind of ice in my veins, at that.

FBI. The very word held terror, images of clandestine

people in black suits who answered to authorities far away. Washington D.C. may have been where I grew up, but its white marble halls of power could not be further removed from the realities of the people who lived there.

Federal bureaus were neighbors to the black neighborhoods of D.C. in the same way an eagle was a neighbor to a mole. We saw each other sometimes. But seeing the feds usually meant that it was time to run and go into hiding.

And yet. And yet. The FBI moving in meant my mother's case was anything but cold. It meant my intuition had been right.

The FBI only got involved when a case crossed state lines, and when the feds really, really wanted it solved. This almost certainly meant that my mother's killer was wanted on other charges. The kinds of charges the feds cared about.

After a moment of dizziness, my heart smiled with a glimpse of hope. I knew the feds would turn a city upside down looking for a suspect. And in this case, I didn't mind.

I had the pen and paper in hand almost before I knew what I was doing. "Could you give me his number, please?"

"Her." My heart skipped a beat. A female federal agent? Maybe, just maybe, she would understand a daughter's plight. I wrote her number down so fast I feared the paper would begin to smoke.

"Thank you, Detective."

"Thank you, Miss Roy. Good luck."

Federal Agent Segal was not an open book. She wouldn't tell me her first name, and I wondered if that was even her real last name. But she listened as I told her what I'd found.

Knowing that just one witness would not be enough, I'd continued working my way down the first-floor hallway and found another family who gave an identical account. None had been willing to talk to the cops, but all were willing to talk to me, the victim's daughter, about what they'd seen and heard.

The yelling and screaming. The gunshots. The small man who held the door and stepped over my mother's body to leave the building.

Segal's silence had a stern quality to it. I could tell she never compromised in anything. She was no automatic friend to me, but she was serious about the investigation. As I talked, I began to breathe a little easier.

"We can't use those witnesses if they won't talk to federal agents," was the first thing she said. "If they won't testify in court, they're almost useless."

I'd been expecting the objection. "They're useless in court, sure. But now *you* know who to look at. You don't need court-admissible testimony for that."

She didn't respond right away. As the silence stretched

on, a horrible thought entered my mind.

What if I was not the only person telling them I had eyewitnesses? What if the Boss and his people were also speaking to the federal agents, giving them incorrect descriptions of the gunmen, throwing them off? What if I was just one of many parties who seemed to have a vested interest in the case—and my own investigation held no more weight than someone else's lies?

"Thank you," Agent Segal said finally. "We'll look into it. Call us if you learn anything new."

We'll look into it.

They needed more. *I* needed more. But where could I get it?

$$$

Hunter was not exactly thrilled to see me. The last time he'd seen my face, I had led his would-be killer into his hospital room while he was too injured to move.

But he loved my mother dearly, and I was her Baby Bear. He knew I would never knowingly cooperate with my mother's killer. And he knew—or hoped—that I'd learned better.

So he opened the screen door of the house where he was staying, in an unknown little neighborhood far from the crime scene. The rented room in an unknown house under an alias was a sort of jury-rigged way of hiding from the people who wanted him dead.

He wasn't in witness protection, because he'd spent weeks refusing to say a word to the investigators. He, too, lived by the code of the streets. And cooperating with the police in any way went against that code.

That was exactly why I came to see him.

It's awkward, to say the least, to have someone welcome you into his home after you almost got him killed.

Hunter was still leaning heavily on a crutch, one knee splinted where a bullet had shattered it. His whole left side had been riddled with bullets, and almost all of the fingers of his left hand had been shot off. It looked painful for him to move. But he was in good spirits, talking and laughing between winces. He seemed to want to pretend that the whole previous episode hadn't happened. And I was only too glad to go along with that.

"Now, Bear," he said as he brought in cookies from the kitchen, "I'm awfully glad to see you. I won't lie; I've been worried. You can't trust anybody around there. Not anybody in your mother's circles. That damn Boss is a fucking snake, and he is not to be trusted."

His words affected me more than I'd expected. I'd known that, been certain of it, for weeks. But the whole time, everybody in the outside world had been telling me I was wrong. To hear someone else state it like a fact hit me hard.

That it was the only man who had *seen* my mother's killers hit me harder.

"Hunter." I opened my mouth perhaps sooner than was polite. He'd barely gotten done easing himself back into the padded armchair that seemed soft enough to soothe his injuries. "I know you know who killed my mother. I know you do."

He looked up from adjusting himself in the chair. "I know you know, Bear. What I'm hoping is that *you* know who it was by now too."

To my utter astonishment, I began to cry. "I know, Hunter," my voice cracked. "It's just—so hard. They were like family to us!"

If he'd had an easier time moving, I think Hunter would have come and sat beside me. As it was, he just kind of leaned forward, one hand half-outstretched.

"I know, Bear. I know it's real fucked up. They killed my woman. The only thing left in my life. But life isn't fair. The streets sure aren't fair. They are dog eat dog, these streets."

"So why won't you testify?" The words exploded out of me. I'd meant to come here about talking to the investigators—nothing more.

Telling an investigator what you know was worlds away from testifying in court, and even that had been a bridge too far. But I knew what I needed. What my mother needed. Her killer would not be charged without *some* eyewitness testimony, and Hunter was the only possible source.

Hunter just kind of froze where he was. He looked like somebody had physically shocked him. He didn't seem to want to move. And I was crying too hard to speak.

"You know I can't do that, Bear," Hunter said finally. But it sounded like it hurt him to say. "I loved your mother. I still do. I'll—" He looked down at himself, seeming suddenly to remember that he was in no condition to take care of her killer himself. "I'll see justice done. But I won't snitch. Your mother wouldn't have wanted me to."

"What 'justice,' Hunter?" I managed. "My mom's not the only one they killed. You know that. And they'd have done more of us if they could. They'd kill me if they knew I was here."

That thought wound him up so much he almost got up out of his chair. He rocked back and forth in it, pushing his good leg against the floor.

"Bear. It's the code I've lived by all my life. We take care of our own problems. We don't involve cops."

"But this is different," I almost shrieked. "My mom's *dead*, Hunter. There was no reason to kill her. You know that. She'd have done anything for the Boss. She loved him like family. He just didn't like that she was—"

I stopped, at a loss for words. What was it I had always sensed, simmering under the too-wide smiles my mother exchanged with the neighbor boy who became the Boss? The fact that she was an independent woman? The fact that she was not under his control?

"No," Hunter said slowly. "You're right. There was no reason Deena should have died. Least of all the way she did. She treated people right, except the ones who didn't treat her family right. They just didn't like that she was smarter than them."

I looked at Hunter, hope and pleading in my eyes. And I knew he saw the same thing I did: that Deena would send down fire from the heavens if her Baby Bear got shot, or followed her mother's footsteps into the world of street justice. And that I wouldn't be able to bear sitting, doing nothing, if the investigators and the courts failed.

Finally, Hunter sighed deeply. "Alright, Bear. Alright. I'll tell them what I know. And if—*if*—they get the right people—I'll testify to what I saw."

THE TRIAL

A criminal investigation can feel endless. This is *especially* true when the case is big. The investigators may have moved sooner on my mother's killer—but they wanted to gather as much evidence as they could.

The Boss and Slim were being looked at for a RICO conspiracy. Under the Racketeering Influence and Corrupt Organizations Act, they could face extra jail time above and beyond what they would face for simple murder.

To build up a RICO case against them, the feds would need to prove that their suspects had been involved in long-term drug trafficking and murder-for-hire as part of an organized crime group.

I didn't know this as the investigation dragged on. I didn't know what was going on behind the scenes. All I knew was that there was no movement that I could see.

My calls to the investigators were weekly, at first. Here's what I've found. Here's who's willing to testify. What have you found? Do you have any new leads?

I realize now that they kept me out of the loop for a reason. Just as I still had not shared my suspicions, or my certainties, with my family, in order to protect them.

For weeks, then months, then *years*, the Boss and his family continued to live across the street from my grandmother. They continued to come to family gatherings, expressing concern. I warned my family to stay away from them—but I dared not tell them why.

What my family didn't know, they could not let slip. As far as they knew, *I* knew nothing. More information about the talk on the streets poured in from friends and neighbors. There were both diversionary tactics and genuine but misguided suspicions.

Some said that a gang from across town had been involved in my mother's murder. Another suggested a man who she had once rejected. I had to pretend that all of these claims were interesting to me. The more confused I looked, the less danger my family was in.

But the game wore on. Long, long. Before I knew it, months had turned into years.

My grandmother became my new rock. For all of the friction between her and my mother, she had nothing but love for me.

Both of us had loved my mother. Both of us had some understanding of the magnitude of the loss. As I watched our family grieve, I began to understand them a little better. They had feared that this end would come for my mother as it had for so many others, and all their disapproval in my childhood had stemmed from their worry.

Uncle Strap wore one of the most devastated faces at my mother's funeral. Whatever his anger, ego, and control issues—it was clear that he really had been trying to protect his baby sister. That he had only strengthened her resolve to bend to no one was a tragedy of its own. People hurt each other so much when they don't know how to listen.

Marquis asked me to marry him. He had become a source of light and stability in my world, keeping Bernard safe as I dipped my toes in dangerous waters. I said, "Yes."

The hurt and emptiness that I felt the day I married him was immeasurable. I barely had the courage and strength it took to walk down the aisle without my mom's presence.

Her absence was tangible. Getting through my wedding day without her smiling with love over my shoulder and giving her blessings was almost impossible.

When Bernard graduated from nursery school, it was a preview of all the other milestones I knew he and I would soon have to face without my mom being here to witness them. I remembered how she used to promise me that she would always be there. That she would always be okay.

I couldn't remember those conversations without a

fresh wave of devastation and heartbreak.

Bernard turned four. Then five. Then six. When I dropped him off for his first day of school, my heart swelled with joy and pride to see my perfect little boy walking through the double doors by himself.

And then it hit me, hard. All of my emotions, feelings of love, excitement, and happiness rolled into one and dissolved into tears. I pressed my face against my hands, crying and screaming.

Because even after three years, my first impulse had been to call my mother and share my feelings with her.

I broke down crying right there in the school parking lot. Reality set in again. I so longed for my mother, and wished she could be here for this crucial milestone in my and my son's lives.

For weeks after my mother died, I'd called her number every day just to hear her recorded voice message. When they disconnected her phone, I fought the urge to keep calling, hoping against hope that she'd pick up.

Twenty-four years' worth of birthdays, Christmases, and Mother's Days served as a reminder that she wasn't there anymore. Always I had the impulse to turn my head and look at her. The expectation that she'd walk into the room any minute now.

Marquis and Bernard did their best to make holidays bearable. I knew that my grief was a burden so big, I could not bear it alone. But I didn't know how to lay it down.

My calls to the investigators became more like monthly. They always assured me they were actively working on the case. They promised me that they were not going to let my mother's murderer get away. That they were still building the case against him.

As the years stretched on, I thought to myself: *This had better be good. You had better be cooking up a case that's worth the wait.*

When the case finally broke, oh Lord. It was.

They finally arrested the Boss's and Slim's asses at a local strip club, where they were caught throwing money in the air all over the naked strippers. That was the last round of dollar bills they would ever throw.

Passing through the security checkpoints at the courthouse was surreal for me. This was not just because my mother's killers were finally being brought to trial after four years of bizarre, agonizing, impenetrable dragging.

It was because it had been four years of pretending that everything was fine, that her murderers were not living free next door to my grandparents, were not continuing to invite me out for drinks and trying to lure me into their car.

Now, the very same people were on trial for my mother's death. I had known, but seeing other people—the FBI and the federal court system, no less—validate my knowledge made it real.

That made the first day of the trial strange and anxious enough. But it got much stranger. Despite my familiarity with courtrooms and the local courthouse, I had never seen anything close to the level of security around my mother's killers.

First, there was the standard courthouse metal detector and X-ray machine. This measure to ensure that no weapons were brought into courtrooms or judge's chambers was normal for all visitors entering the building.

But as I walked down the white-tiled halls toward the courtroom where the Boss and Slim were being tried, I was greeted by a surprise.

There was *another* metal detector that I had to go through, followed by another checkpoint, an extra search-and-frisk procedure that I had to submit to before entering the courtroom itself. In case anyone had managed to smuggle weapons through the first checkpoint, I supposed.

As I finally stepped over the threshold into the courtroom, my jaw dropped. This courtroom had a feature I'd never seen before, even in the most lurid and sensationalist television dramas.

A thick wall of bulletproof plexiglass ran from floor to ceiling, separating the defendants and defense witnesses from the judge and the prosecution.

I was already shaking, my heart pounding at the question of what these extra measures meant, when the Boss and Slim were brought out. I was already considering what, exactly, I had been living next to for so many years.

And the surprises weren't over yet.

The Boss and Slim were wearing actual, literal chains around their wrists and ankles that forced them to shuffle as they walked. There was something black and thick fixed around each of their waists—an electric shock belt, I realized, feeling queasy. These men did not just warrant bulletproof glass and chains separating them from their accusers: the court needed the ability to incapacitate them from a distance at any time.

Any temptation the jury may have had to feel sorry for these men was erased by one thing: their smiles.

Far from looking frightened or oppressed, the Boss and Slim were smiling smugly. Cruelly. They'd dressed in their 9-5 business suits and ties and put on glasses. They were clearly trying to present themselves as studious businessmen—not ruthless killers!

To me, it looked as though they were more proud of the accomplishments that brought them here. As though they were certain that the court would not convict them—far more certain than an innocent man who'd been wrongly accused would have been.

As their eyes scanned the courtroom, the Boss's eyes lingered on me. His grin widened, showing his teeth. Taunting me.

I was pissed, hurt, angry. Every emotion you could think of ran through me. I wanted to kill them myself. The force of it almost doubled me over with pain. I remembered my mother's explosive smile, and that she would never smile it again.

My mind was racing, and the pit of my stomach dropped out.

How dangerous, exactly, were these family friends? My neighbors, who I'd grown up across the street from? If what I was seeing was any indication, these friends and neighbors had certainly killed my mother in cold blood. But for the court to treat these men as though they posed a danger to the entire criminal justice system—

How many *other* people had they murdered?

Hundreds, the prosecution claimed, across the weeks and months of the trial. And we who knew them, who knew how the streets worked, believed them. But the courts could only prove 35 of the murders.

What I had seen so far suggested that the court and the defendants agreed on one thing: that these men might be *too* dangerous to prosecute. That their friends might find a way to threaten the judge, the jury, the defense witnesses and their families. That they might gain their freedom, not through innocence, but through a level of power through violence that strained credulity.

That they'd done it before.

Was there any possibility that these fears were *right*? Was there any possibility of a wrongful acquittal?

I felt sick at the very thought of these men walking free. Of my mother's killers going unpunished.

At last the opening ceremonies concluded, and the trial commenced. These were to be the longest months of my life.

I attended the first ten months of the hearings alone. I'd leave work an hour early every day in order to be present for as much of the proceeding as possible.

My colleagues understood. My employer knew the whole story: that my beloved mother had been brutally murdered, that no suspect had been brought to trial for four years, that I had been waiting for this trial for a significant portion of my life. No one was going to stop me from being present at this trial, from hearing everything the prosecution had found about my mother's killers.

But I did not invite my family. Not yet.

This was not because I thought it wasn't worth their time, or I wanted to keep the trial to myself. I would have loved to have my cousins, aunts, and uncles in the trenches with me daily.

The truth was, I feared for their safety, if the court was so utterly terrified of these men. With their families still living next door to my own, I dare not start conversations about their guilt or innocence in the neighborhood. I dare not create the barest suggestion that anyone in my family could, conceivably, be suspected of planning to testify.

So I sat alone in the courtroom, alongside reporters and allies of the Boss and Slim. I knew their faces from my neighborhood and my mother's kitchen table. Members of their operation would secretly sit in the back corners, so they could sneak in and out without being noticed by the court officers or reporters.

I felt like a creature out of time, sitting among enemies as the evidence was brought out. There were boxes of it. Truckloads of it.

Under the smiling eyes of the Boss and Slim, 35 different guns—each ballistically matched to at least one murder—were presented to the court.

The prosecution told the jury that over 200 murders were represented by these 35 guns. I could believe it. Everyone who knew the streets could believe it.

As the investigators spoke, a chilling picture of my neighbors emerged.

The Boss had climbed swiftly through the criminal underground during our shared youth—in part because of his tremendous willingness and skillfulness in murder. Whether my mother had known quite *why* he was considered so useful and respected was unclear, but his simple approach to solving problems—by killing the person causing them—made him a useful asset to any ruthless drug lord.

His apparent total lack of conscience or remorse allowed him to arrogantly shrug off any concerns, even pretending to be a confused family friend or a traumatized witness. He did this so convincingly that he had escaped prosecution while racking up a body count that approached the world record for known serial killers. He took out rivals and friends alike when they became too powerful or became suspected liabilities.

I thought about him leaning over Hunter in the hospital room, and my heart ached as I struggled for breath. His confidence in threatening a man inside a medical facility, surrounded by security cameras and medical staff, had always been astounding to me.

Would he have shot Hunter then and there, if the nurse had not interrupted us? Would he have done the same to Andrea Prince and me, if there had been any other witnesses?

Would he have gotten away with it? Had he done it before?

Among the possessions recovered from the Boss's house in a raid was a copy of *The Godfather*.

The same movie my mother had watched, cultivating her street persona, while I was a small child. The movie that had helped inspire her to seek power outside the law—and to live by the sword, knowing she may well die by it.

Finally, after grueling months of testimony from dozens of witnesses and forensic experts, I was sure that the suspects would be convicted. No one from the defense team or the jury had dropped dead or disappeared. As the months passed and clearly terrified witnesses testified anyway, the Boss and Slim's smiles had begun to waver.

On the day that the verdict was due, I called my family to come to the courthouse.

I was expected to deliver a victim's impact statement.

These statements are a final plea to the judge to request the harshest possible sentence for the perpetrators. My statement would express to the judge and jury how the senseless murder of my mother had impacted me, and the lives of my family members.

Over a dozen of Lady D's siblings, nieces and nephews turned out to support me. We all listened and watched the final proceedings with wide eyes and pounding hearts. My grandmother, who was then in her nineties, attended. She watched with a trembling lip as the neighbor boy she'd known since he was born was convicted of killing her daughter in cold blood.

Finally, I took the stand. I had difficulty keeping my composure as I spoke of the pain of going through life milestones without my mother. Of all she had meant to me, and all she had done for me—and of waking up in the morning knowing that my mother was not breathing.

I painted for the courtroom, as vividly as I could, the image of my mother. A woman who would do anything to protect her family. And the image of the aching hole her absence left in all our hearts.

As I gave my victim's impact statement, there wasn't a dry eye in the courtroom. I know the judges and prosecutors are trained to keep a straight face without showing emotion or remorse, but they couldn't.

As I spoke, the judge's face turned deep red. As his eyes filled up with tears that never fell, I knew that my impact statement would touch the hearts of all those who could relate. All those who had a daughter, or a mom, would be able to empathize with the pain I was feeling.

Slowly, after what seemed an interminable wait, the verdict was read.

A cheer went up in the spectators' box as the defendants were found guilty on over 200 criminal charges.

12

Nothing in life is ever easy. This is true with justice, as it is with anything else.

My mother's killers were convicted and received 100 consecutive life sentences each. They did not go free, and they will never see the light of day again.

But they were denied the death penalty, despite the dozens of lives they themselves have taken.

That stung my family deeply. To this day, the Boss and Slim can wake up in their cells and draw breath. They can stare at the ceiling, and I wouldn't put it past them to be pulling strings from inside the prison.

My mother can't even draw breath. She cannot open her eyes to see her daughter and grandson's loving faces.

The feeling that this is an injustice is universal in the family.

While we understand opposition to the death penalty on the grounds that some who are convicted are innocent, there is no shadow of a reasonable doubt as to who killed my mother. Or countless other people, every one of them beloved, who crossed the paths of two men who liked nothing better than to play God.

These men do not deserve to live. They do not deserve to have our tax dollars spent on them, feeding them and clothing them. They do not deserve the chance to do more violence, which the record of their lives has shown to be their constant pattern of behavior. Nobody is benefitted by keeping them alive.

But we live with the reality we have. And in the meantime, life goes on.

My precious Bernard has grown into a man whom I am very proud of as the years have passed. Though he and his half-brother have never formed a close bond, he is a happy young man who knows that his family always has his back.

I've cried at his countless graduations, basketball games, and other proud achievements—in part because my joyous pride always came with the reminder that I could not share it with my mother.

After eighteen years, Marquis and I are no longer married—but that's another story, for another time. Another book, perhaps. My slow exploration of my sexuality after my childhood abuse is a subject worthy of its own discussion.

This book is about Lady D, my mother.

Grief never really goes away. Anyone who's lost a parent or child in an untimely matter knows this. It stays with you, and you grow around it.

But it can evolve.

As the years pass, I've struggled to come to terms with my mother's absence. That one vibrant, loving presence who supported me and taught me joy for the first 21 years of my life is missing. She's missing from my life, and the life of my son.

But she is not *just* missing.

I don't make any claims to know about the afterlife or its exact nature. But I know that I have felt my mother's presence, heard her speak in my heart at my life's major milestones. In time, the grief of loss has given way to a new kind of understanding. My mother isn't where I'd like her to be, but she is *somewhere.* And she can see us.

I'm not the only one who feels her.

Years after the Boss's sentencing, Lady D's family gathered from far and wide to face a solemn responsibility. My grandmother, the matriarch of the family, had finally passed away after living to be nearly 100 years old. Her house—the house that countless children and grandchildren had grown up in—now needed to be passed down to a younger couple who were looking to start a family.

The memories that lay over that house weighed heavily on us. There were so many memories of good times, of the formative years of our upbringing with family. But even these were made bittersweet by the untimely death of my mother, the center of life and laughter in that house for so many years.

And there were the bad memories. I don't know how many other people in the family had memories like mine of Uncle Strap or Cousin Bigelow living in that house, but the feeling that hung over us as we gathered was not all sweetness and light. We knew what had to be done.

Over the course of weeks and months, we cleaned the house, emptying it of my grandmother and grandfather's belongings. We apportioned them among ourselves, or to other good homes who we knew my grandparents would have wanted to inherit these relics.

We did renovations and maintenance. Where there were things we couldn't fix, we called in contractors to make the house as bright and sturdy and spotless as it had been the day my grandparents first bought it, proud black homeowners in what was then a prosperous neighborhood, nearly a century ago.

When we passed the house down to a brand-new couple looking to start a family together, we gathered one last time to reminisce and say our final goodbyes.

As we stood in the backyard of an auntie's house eating barbecue, cousin Killa stood near me, his eyes shining with tears.

"Deena's looking down on us," he said. "She's smiling. I swear I heard her say we did a good job. She's proud that we stuck together."

As Killa spoke, the sun broke through the clouds. White doves fluttered through the sky above, growing thicker as the afternoon wore on. I knew that Killa was right: my mom was smiling down on us.

I looked up to see that the clouds were silver-lined, and sunbeams were spilling down onto the family.

At that moment, I felt my heart smile. Part of my spirit sprouted wings and flew to see my mother. Wherever she may be.

Made in the USA
Middletown, DE
09 July 2020